Linux Decoded

A Comprehensive Linux Command Line and Shell Scripting Handbook

Robert Frangias

Contents

Welcome to the Command Line

1

You're about to step into a different way of interacting with computers, a place where typed commands unlock immense power and flexibility. This realm is the Linux command line, often called the *terminal* or *shell*. While graphical interfaces with icons and menus are familiar, the command line is the true heart of Linux, offering a direct line to the system's core. It might seem a bit mysterious at first, perhaps even intimidating, but stick with me. By the end of this journey, you'll wield the command line with confidence, automating tasks and understanding Linux on a much deeper level. This chapter is your first step, helping you get acquainted with this fascinating environment.

What is Linux, Really?

Before we dive into commands, let's briefly talk about Linux itself. What *is* it? At its core, Linux is technically just the **kernel** – the central part of the operating system that manages the computer's hardware and allows software to run. Think of the kernel as the engine of a car.

However, when people talk about "Linux," they usually mean a complete operating system built *around* the Linux kernel. This includes the kernel plus a collection of system software, utilities, and often a graphical desktop environment. These complete packages are called **Linux distributions** (or "distros"). Popular examples include Ubuntu, Fedora, Debian, CentOS, Arch Linux, and many more.

Linux has a rich history rooted in the early 1990s, started by Linus Torvalds as a personal project. It was heavily inspired by an older operating system called UNIX. A key part of the Linux story is its connection to the **GNU Project**, which provided many of the essential command-line tools and system libraries needed to make a usable operating system around the Linux kernel.

Perhaps the most defining characteristic of Linux is its **open-source** nature. This means its underlying source code is freely available for anyone to view, modify, and share. This philosophy has fostered a massive global community of developers and users who collaborate to improve and extend the system. It's built on principles of freedom, sharing, and transparency, which is a big part of why many people are so passionate about it.

Why Bother with the Command Line?

In a world of slick graphical user interfaces (GUIs), why learn the command line? It's a fair question! GUIs are often intuitive for simple tasks like opening a file or browsing the web. However, the command line offers distinct advantages, especially as you delve deeper into Linux:

1. **Power and Flexibility:** You can often perform complex tasks with a single command that would require many clicks in a GUI. Combining commands allows for intricate operations.
2. **Efficiency:** For experienced users, typing commands is frequently faster than navigating menus and clicking icons. Keyboard shortcuts and command history further speed things up.
3. **Automation:** This is a huge one! The command line is the foundation of **shell scripting** (which we'll explore thoroughly later in this book). You can write scripts to automate repetitive tasks, saving you immense amounts of time and effort.
4. **Remote Access:** When managing servers or systems remotely, you'll almost always connect via a command-line interface (like SSH, which we'll touch on later). GUIs aren't always available or practical in these scenarios.
5. **Resource Usage:** Command-line interfaces generally use fewer system resources (memory, CPU) than graphical environments. This is crucial on sys-

tems with limited resources or when you need maximum performance for other tasks.

6. **Deeper Understanding:** Working at the command line gives you a much clearer picture of how the operating system actually works under the hood.

Think of it like driving a car. A GUI is like an automatic transmission – easy to get started with and handles many situations well. The command line is like a manual transmission – it requires a bit more skill initially, but it gives you finer control, better performance (in some contexts), and a deeper connection to the machine. Both have their place, but mastering the manual (the command line) opens up new possibilities.

Understanding the Shell

When you open a terminal window, you're not interacting directly with the Linux kernel. Instead, you're interacting with a program called the **shell**.

The shell acts as an **interpreter**. It takes the commands you type, figures out what you mean, and then asks the kernel or other programs to carry out the actions. It also takes the output from those programs and displays it back to you in the terminal. It's the crucial intermediary between you and the operating system's core.

Imagine you're visiting a foreign country where you don't speak the language (the kernel's language). The shell is your fluent interpreter, translating your requests into the local language and relaying the responses back to you.

Meet the Popular Shells

There isn't just one shell; Linux offers several options, each with slightly different features and behaviors. Here are some of the most common ones:

- **Bash (Bourne Again SHell):** This is the most widely used and the default shell on the vast majority of Linux distributions and even macOS. It's powerful, feature-rich, and what we'll focus on throughout this book because of its prevalence. If you learn Bash, you'll be comfortable on almost any Linux system.
- **Zsh (Z Shell):** A very popular alternative to Bash, known for its extensive customization options, improved tab completion, spelling correction, and plugin support (like the famous "Oh My Zsh" framework).
- **Fish (Friendly Interactive SHell):** Aims to be particularly user-friendly out-of-the-box, with features like syntax highlighting and autosuggestions built-in, requiring less configuration than Bash or Zsh.

- **Ksh (KornShell):** An older shell, influential in Bash's development, still used in some enterprise UNIX environments.
- **Csh / Tcsh:** Shells with syntax more similar to the C programming language. Less common for interactive use today compared to Bash or Zsh.

While these others exist and have their fans, **we will focus exclusively on Bash**. Its commands and scripting syntax are the de facto standard in many contexts, making it the most practical choice for a comprehensive introduction. The core concepts you learn with Bash are also transferable if you decide to explore other shells later.

Opening Your First Terminal Window

Okay, enough theory! Let's get our hands dirty. How do you actually start a terminal session? The exact method depends on the Linux distribution and the desktop environment you're using (like GNOME, KDE, XFCE, etc.), but here are the common ways:

1. **Look for an Icon:** Most graphical desktops have an icon that looks like a black screen or monitor, often with a > or $ symbol on it. It might be in your application menu (often under "System Tools," "Utilities," or "Accessories") or pinned to a dock or panel. Common names include "Terminal," "Console," "Konsole" (KDE), or "GNOME Terminal."
2. **Use a Keyboard Shortcut:** Many systems have a shortcut like Ctrl+Alt+T configured to launch a terminal instantly. Try it!
3. **Use the Search Function:** Most modern desktops have a search bar (often accessible by pressing the Super key, which is usually the Windows key on most keyboards). Just type "terminal" and it should pop up.

Once you launch it, you'll typically see a window containing a **prompt**. It might look something like this:

```
your_username@your_hostname:~$
```

Or perhaps:

```
[your_username@your_hostname ~]$
```

This prompt is the shell's way of saying, "I'm ready for your command." The exact appearance varies, but it usually shows your username, the system's name (hostname), and your current location in the filesystem (we'll cover the ~ symbol in the next chapter). The $ symbol generally indicates you're logged in as a regular user (a # symbol usually means you're the powerful *root* user – more on that in Chapter 5).

Go ahead, type something simple like date and press Enter.

```
$ date
Tue Jul 23 10:30:15 EDT 2024
```

See? You just gave the shell a command (date), it understood, executed the corresponding program, and showed you the output (the current date and time). You're commanding Linux!

The Anatomy of a Command

You just ran the date command. That was a very simple one. Most commands follow a standard structure:

```
command [options] [arguments]
```

Let's break this down:

1. **Command:** This is the name of the program you want to run (like date, ls, cd, cp). It's almost always the first thing on the line and is **case-sensitive** (ls is different from LS).
2. **Options (or Flags):** These modify the command's behavior. They usually start with one hyphen (-) for short, single-letter options (e.g., -l) or two hyphens (--) for longer, more descriptive options (e.g., --human-readable). You can often combine multiple short options (e.g., -la is the same as -l -a). Options are, well, *optional*.
3. **Arguments:** These specify *what* the command should act upon, like a filename, a directory name, or some text. Not all commands require arguments. For example, date doesn't need any.

Let's look at a slightly more complex example using the ls command (which lists directory contents):

```
$ ls -l /home/your_username
```

- ls: This is the **command.**

- -l: This is an **option** telling ls to use a "long" listing format, showing more details.
- /home/your_username: This is the **argument**, specifying the directory whose contents ls should list. (Replace your_username with your actual username).

Understanding this structure is fundamental. As you learn new commands, pay attention to the options and arguments they accept.

Getting Help When You're Stuck

No one remembers every command and every option – not even seasoned veterans! Thankfully, Linux provides excellent built-in help systems. Knowing how to find help is one of the most crucial skills you can learn.

The Manual (man)

The primary source of documentation is the manual pages, accessed with the man command. To get help for a specific command, just type man followed by the command name.

```
$ man ls
```

This will open the manual page for the ls command within a pager program (usually less, which we'll meet properly in Chapter 4). You'll see:

- **NAME:** The command name and a brief description.
- **SYNOPSIS:** How to use the command, showing options and arguments. Square brackets [] usually indicate optional items.
- **DESCRIPTION:** A detailed explanation of what the command does.
- **OPTIONS:** A list of available options and what they do.
- **EXAMPLES:** Practical usage examples.
- **SEE ALSO:** Related commands or topics.
- ...and sometimes more sections like Files, Author, Bugs.

Navigating man **pages:**

- Use the **Arrow keys** (Up/Down) or **Page Up/Page Down** keys to scroll.
- Type / followed by a keyword and press Enter to search forward for that keyword. Type n to find the next occurrence.
- Type ? followed by a keyword and press Enter to search backward.
- Press h for a help screen summarizing navigation commands.

- Press q to **quit** the man page viewer and return to your shell prompt.

Get into the habit of consulting the man pages whenever you encounter a new command or forget how an option works. It's your best friend on the command line.

Info Pages (info)

Some programs, particularly those from the GNU project, provide documentation in the info format, which is designed to be structured like a hypertext document.

```
$ info coreutils ls invocation
```

Info pages can be more detailed or structured differently than man pages. Navigation is slightly different (using commands like n for next node, p for previous, u for up, m for menu selection). Honestly, many people find info less intuitive than man initially, but it's good to know it exists, as some commands have more extensive documentation there. Press q to quit.

The Help Option (--help)

Many commands also offer a quick summary of their options directly via a --help option. This is often faster than opening the full man page if you just need a quick reminder.

```
$ ls --help
Usage: ls [OPTION]... [FILE]...
List information about the FILEs (the current directory by default).
Sort entries alphabetically if none of -cftuvSUX nor --sort is specified.

Mandatory arguments to long options are mandatory for short options too.
  -a, --all                  do not ignore entries starting with .
  -A, --almost-all           do not list implied . and ..
      --author               with -l, print the author of each file
  -b, --escape               print C-style escapes for nongraphic characters
      --block-size=SIZE      with -l, scale sizes by SIZE when printing them;
                               e.g., '--block-size=M'; see SIZE format below
  -B, --ignore-backups       do not list implied entries ending with ~
  -c                         with -lt: sort by, and show, ctime (time of last
                               modification of file status information);
                               with -l: show ctime and sort by name;
                               otherwise: sort by ctime, newest first
...
*output truncated for brevity*
```

The output is usually less detailed than man but provides a handy synopsis and option list directly in your terminal.

Don't feel overwhelmed! The key is knowing *how* to find the information you need using man or --help.

Chapter Summary

We've taken our first exciting steps into the Linux command line! You now understand that Linux is more than just a kernel, it's a complete operating system often packaged as a distribution. We explored *why* the command line remains so relevant and powerful compared to graphical interfaces. You met the **shell**, specifically **Bash**, which acts as your interpreter, translating your typed commands into actions. We saw how to open a terminal window and interact with the prompt. Critically, you learned the basic structure of a command (command [options] [arguments]) and, most importantly, how to use man, info, and --help to get assistance when you need it.

You've laid the groundwork. Now that you know how to issue basic commands and find help, it's time to learn how to move around within the Linux system. In the next chapter, we'll explore the Linux filesystem structure and learn the essential commands for navigating directories.

2

Navigating Your Linux Filesystem

In the previous chapter, you got your first taste of the command line, learning how to issue commands and seek help when needed. Now, it's time to explore the landscape where these commands operate: the Linux filesystem. Think of the filesystem as a vast, organized digital filing cabinet. Knowing how to find your way around this structure is fundamental to using Linux effectively. In this chapter, we'll become digital explorers, learning how to identify our current location, move between different areas, and see what's inside them.

The Linux Directory Tree

Unlike operating systems that might use separate drive letters (like C: or D:), Linux organizes everything under a single, unified structure called a **directory tree**. It all starts from the top, a special directory known simply as **root**, represented by a forward slash (/). Every single file and directory on your Linux system resides somewhere under this root directory.

Imagine an upside-down tree. The / is the base of the trunk, and all other directories branch out from it. These branches can contain files or further sub-directories (more branches). This hierarchical structure is key to keeping things organized.

While exploring, you'll encounter many standard directories directly under /. Their existence isn't random; it follows a convention called the **Filesystem Hierarchy Standard (FHS)**, which helps ensure that programs know where to find things across different Linux distributions. You don't need to memorize every detail right now, but getting familiar with the purpose of a few key top-level directories is incredibly helpful:

- / (Root): The top level, the starting point for everything.
- /bin: Contains essential **bin**ary executables (basic commands like `ls`, `cp`, `mv`) needed by both the system administrator and regular users, available even if nothing else is mounted.
- /sbin: Holds essential **s**ystem **bin**aries, primarily used for system administration tasks (like `fdisk`, `reboot`). Regular users might not run these directly.
- /etc: The configuration hub. This directory contains system-wide configuration **etc**etera files for the operating system and many installed applications. You'll often edit files here (carefully!) to customize system behavior.
- /home: Where user **home** directories live. Each user typically gets their own directory here (e.g., /home/alice, /home/bob) to store personal files, documents, and user-specific configurations. This is likely where you'll spend most of your time.
- /var: Holds **var**iable data files. This includes things that change frequently, like system logs (/var/log), mail spools, printer queues, and temporary files used by databases.
- /tmp: A place for **temp**orary files. Programs (and users) can store files here that aren't needed long-term. Often, the contents of /tmp are cleared out when the system reboots.
- /usr: Contains **U**nix **S**ystem **R**esources. This is a large directory hierarchy containing non-essential user programs (/usr/bin), libraries (/usr/lib), documentation (/usr/share/doc), and source code (/usr/src). Think of it as the place for installed software and its supporting files.
- /boot: Contains files needed for the system's **boot** process, including the Linux kernel itself. You generally won't need to touch files here unless you're doing advanced system configuration.
- /dev: Contains **dev**ice files. Linux treats hardware devices (like hard drives, keyboards, printers) as files. These special files provide a way for programs to interact with hardware.

This isn't an exhaustive list, but it covers the most important directories you'll encounter initially. Just remember the core idea: everything starts at / and branches out logically.

Finding Your Way

When navigating a large city, you occasionally need to check a map to see "You Are Here." In the Linux filesystem, the command for this is pwd, which stands for **print working directory.**

It's incredibly simple to use. Just type pwd and press Enter:

```
$ pwd
/home/your_username
```

The shell responds by printing the **full path** to the directory you are currently in. The path shows the sequence of directories starting from the root (/) down to your current location, separated by forward slashes. In this example, you are in the your_username directory, which is inside the /home directory, which is directly under the root (/) directory.

Use pwd whenever you feel unsure about your current location in the directory tree. It's your reliable compass.

Moving Around

Knowing where you are is useful, but you also need to move around! The command for changing your current location is cd, which stands for **change directory.** It's one of the most frequently used commands.

The cd command takes one main argument: the directory you want to move *to*. The way you specify this destination directory is crucial, and there are two primary methods: using absolute paths and relative paths.

Absolute Paths

An **absolute path** specifies a location starting from the very top – the root directory (/). It's like giving a complete street address, including the country, city, street, and house number. It works no matter where you currently are in the filesystem because it always starts from the known beginning (/).

For example, to move to the system configuration directory /etc, you would use its absolute path:

```
$ pwd
/home/your_username
$ cd /etc
$ pwd
/etc
```

Notice how after running `cd /etc`, the `pwd` command confirms you are now in the /etc directory.

To move back to your home directory using its absolute path (assuming your username is `jane`):

```
$ pwd
/etc
$ cd /home/jane
$ pwd
/home/jane
```

Absolute paths are unambiguous but can sometimes be long to type.

Relative Paths

A **relative path** specifies a location *relative* to your current working directory. It's like giving directions based on where you are right now: "go down the hall and take the first door on the left." Relative paths *do not* start with a forward slash (/).

Let's say you are in your home directory (/home/jane) and it contains a subdirectory named `Documents`. To move into `Documents`, you can use a relative path:

```
$ pwd
/home/jane
$ ls
Desktop  Documents  Downloads  Music  Pictures  Public  Templates  Videos
$ cd Documents
$ pwd
/home/jane/Documents
```

You simply provided the name of the subdirectory within your current location.

Now, imagine `Documents` contains another subdirectory called `Projects`. You can move into it similarly:

```
$ pwd
/home/jane/Documents
$ ls
file1.txt  report.odt  Projects
$ cd Projects
$ pwd
/home/jane/Documents/Projects
```

Relative paths are often shorter to type than absolute paths, especially when moving to nearby directories. However, **they only work correctly based on your current location**. If you tried running cd Documents while you were in /etc, it wouldn't work because there (probably) isn't a subdirectory named Documents inside /etc.

Special Directories

To make navigation even easier, the shell understands several special directory notations:

- **.** (A single dot): This represents the **current directory** itself. It might seem redundant, but it's occasionally useful in commands and scripts. For example, cd . technically changes directory to where you already are – not very useful on its own, but the concept is important.

- **..** (Two dots): This represents the **parent directory** – the directory one level *up* from your current location. This is incredibly useful for moving back up the tree.

  ```
  $ pwd
  /home/jane/Documents/Projects
  $ cd ..
  $ pwd
  /home/jane/Documents
  $ cd ..
  $ pwd
  /home/jane
  ```

  Each cd .. moves you one level higher in the hierarchy.

- **~** (Tilde): This is a shortcut for your **home directory**. No matter where you are in the filesystem, typing cd ~ will always take you back to your personal home directory. Even simpler, typing cd with **no arguments** at all usually does the same thing!

```
$ pwd
/var/log
$ cd ~
$ pwd
/home/jane
$ cd /tmp
$ pwd
/tmp
$ cd
$ pwd
/home/jane
```

The tilde (~) is a fantastic time-saver. You can also use it as part of a longer path, for example, cd ~/Documents/Projects.

- – (Hyphen): This special character represents the **previous working directory** you were in. It's like the "back" button in a web browser for your directory history.

```
$ pwd
/home/jane/Documents
$ cd /etc
$ pwd
/etc
$ cd -
/home/jane/Documents
$ pwd
/home/jane/Documents
$ cd -
/etc
$ pwd
/etc
```

Each cd - swaps you back to the directory you were in just before the current one. The shell even prints the name of the directory it's taking you to.

Mastering cd with absolute paths, relative paths, and these special shortcuts (. ., ~, -) is essential for efficient command-line navigation. Practice moving around between /, your home directory, /etc, and any subdirectories you create.

Listing Files and Directories

Once you've navigated to a directory using cd, you'll want to see what's inside it. The command for this is ls, which **lists** directory contents.

In its simplest form, just type ls:

```
$ pwd
/home/jane
$ ls
Desktop  Documents  Downloads  Music  Pictures  Public  Templates  Videos
```

By default, ls lists the names of files and subdirectories within the current working directory, usually sorted alphabetically. It often uses colors to differentiate between file types (e.g., blue for directories, white for regular files), but this depends on your terminal configuration.

Like most Linux commands, ls becomes much more informative with options. Here are some of the most common and useful ones:

- -l (Long Listing Format): This option provides much more detail about each item.

  ```
  $ ls -l
  total 32
  drwxr-xr-x 2 jane users 4096 Jul 20 11:15 Desktop
  drwxr-xr-x 3 jane users 4096 Jul 23 09:40 Documents
  drwxr-xr-x 2 jane users 4096 Jul 20 11:15 Downloads
  drwxr-xr-x 2 jane users 4096 Jul 20 11:15 Music
  drwxr-xr-x 2 jane users 4096 Jul 20 11:15 Pictures
  drwxr-xr-x 2 jane users 4096 Jul 20 11:15 Public
  drwxr-xr-x 2 jane users 4096 Jul 20 11:15 Templates
  drwxr-xr-x 2 jane users 4096 Jul 20 11:15 Videos
  ```

  We'll break down this output in the next section.

- -a (All): By default, ls hides files and directories whose names begin with a dot (.). These are often configuration files or special directories. The -a option tells ls to show *all* entries, including hidden ones.

  ```
  $ ls -a
  .    .bash_history  .config  Documents  Music     Public     Videos
  ..   .bash_logout   Desktop  Downloads  Pictures  Templates  .viminfo
  ```

```
.bashrc .cache    .local    .profile
```

Notice the appearance of . (current directory) and .. (parent directory), as well as several hidden configuration files like .bashrc and .profile.

- -h (Human-Readable): When used with -l, this option displays file sizes in a more human-friendly format (e.g., 4.0K for kilobytes, 1.2M for megabytes) instead of just plain bytes. This makes it much easier to gauge file sizes quickly.

```
$ # First, let's create a slightly larger file for demonstration
$ head -c 5000000 /dev/urandom > big_file.dat
$ ls -lh
total 4.9M
-rw-r--r-- 1 jane users 4.8M Jul 23 11:05 big_file.dat
drwxr-xr-x 2 jane users 4.0K Jul 20 11:15 Desktop
drwxr-xr-x 3 jane users 4.0K Jul 23 09:40 Documents
drwxr-xr-x 2 jane users 4.0K Jul 20 11:15 Downloads
drwxr-xr-x 2 jane users 4.0K Jul 20 11:15 Music
drwxr-xr-x 2 jane users 4.0K Jul 20 11:15 Pictures
drwxr-xr-x 2 jane users 4.0K Jul 20 11:15 Public
drwxr-xr-x 2 jane users 4.0K Jul 20 11:15 Templates
drwxr-xr-x 2 jane users 4.0K Jul 20 11:15 Videos
```

See how big_file.dat shows 4.8M instead of a large number like 5000000? Much easier to read!

- -t (Time): Sorts the output by modification time, showing the newest items first.

- -r (Reverse): Reverses the order of the sort. For example, ls -ltr will show the *oldest* items last in a long, time-sorted format (a very common combination).

You can combine options. For instance, ls -alh shows all files (including hidden), in long format, with human-readable sizes. Experiment with these options to see how they change the output. Remember, man ls is your friend if you want to explore the many other options available!

Understanding ls -l Output

The long listing format (ls -l) provides a wealth of information. Let's break down a typical line:

`drwxr-xr-x 3 jane users 4096 Jul 23 09:40 Documents`

1. **File Type and Permissions** (`drwxr-xr-x`):
   - The very first character indicates the file type:
     - d: Directory
     - -: Regular file
     - l: Symbolic link (a shortcut to another file/directory)
     - Others exist (c, b for devices), but these are the most common.
   - The next nine characters represent the **permissions** for the file, broken into three sets of three:
     - rwx: Permissions for the **owner** (Read, Write, Execute)
     - r-x: Permissions for the **group** (Read, Execute, no Write)
     - r-x: Permissions for **others** (Read, Execute, no Write)
   - Don't worry about memorizing permissions right now; we'll dedicate a significant part of **Chapter 5** to understanding and changing these.

2. **Number of Hard Links** (3): For files, this is usually 1. For directories, it's the number of subdirectories plus . and .. (Hard links are an advanced topic we won't focus on now).

3. **Owner** (jane): The username of the user who owns the file or directory.

4. **Group** (users): The name of the group that owns the file or directory.

5. **Size** (4096): The size of the file in bytes (or a human-readable format if -h is used). For directories, this size is often related to the space needed to store the list of files inside it, not the total size of its contents.

6. **Last Modification Time** (Jul 23 09:40): The date and time the file's content was last modified.

7. **Name** (Documents): The name of the file or directory.

Looking at the `ls -l` output carefully tells you a lot about the items in a directory beyond just their names.

Speeding Things Up

Okay, typing all those directory and command names can get tedious, and typos are easy to make. This is where one of the shell's most helpful features comes in: **Tab Completion**.

Bash (and most modern shells) can automatically complete commands, filenames, and directory names for you. Start typing the beginning of a name and then press the Tab key.

- **Unique Completion:** If there's only one possible way to complete what you've typed, the shell will fill in the rest of the name automatically.

```
$ pwd
/home/jane
$ ls
Desktop  Documents  Downloads  Music  Pictures  Public  Templates
Videos
$ cd Docu<Tab>
```

After pressing Tab, the shell completes it to:

```
$ cd Documents/
```

Notice it even adds the trailing slash for a directory!

- **Multiple Possibilities:** If multiple names start with what you've typed, pressing Tab once might do nothing or just beep. Press Tab a *second* time, and the shell will list all the possible completions.

```
$ pwd
/home/jane
$ cd D<Tab><Tab>
Desktop/   Documents/ Downloads/
$ cd D
```

After pressing Tab twice, it shows the options starting with D. You can then type another letter (e.g., o) and press Tab again for unique completion.

```
$ cd Do<Tab>
$ cd Documents/
```

- **Command Completion:** Tab completion also works for command names themselves.

```
$ mkd<Tab><Tab>
mkdep   mkdir   mkdict   mkfifo   mkfontdir
$ mkd
```

Tab completion is more than just a convenience; it's a fundamental technique for working efficiently and accurately on the command line. It reduces typing, prevents errors caused by misspelling names, and helps you discover files or commands when you only remember the first part of their name. **Use it constantly!** Make pressing the Tab key a reflex action whenever you're typing paths or commands.

Chapter Summary

You've now become a navigator of the Linux filesystem! We explored the hierarchical directory tree starting from the root (/) and learned the purpose of key standard directories like /etc, /home, and /bin. You learned how to pinpoint your current location using pwd and, crucially, how to move around using cd with both absolute and relative paths, along with the handy shortcuts .., ~, and -. We then covered how to list directory contents with ls and its powerful options like -l, -a, and -h, even deciphering the detailed output of ls -l. Finally, you discovered the indispensable time-saver: Tab completion.

With the ability to navigate and view the filesystem, you're ready for the next logical step. Now that you can find your way around and see what's there, you'll want to start creating, organizing, and managing your own files and directories. In the next chapter, we'll dive into commands like touch, mkdir, cp, mv, and rm – the essential tools for file manipulation.

3

Managing Files and Directories

Alright, you've learned how to navigate the Linux filesystem like a seasoned explorer using `pwd`, `cd`, and `ls`, as we saw in Chapter 2. You can find your way around and see what's inside directories. But what about creating your own landmarks? How do you organize your digital space, copy important documents, rename files, or clear out clutter? That's exactly what this chapter is about. We'll equip you with the essential tools for managing files and directories – creating them, copying, moving, renaming, and yes, even deleting them (carefully!). We'll also introduce a powerful concept called wildcards to handle multiple files at once.

To practice these commands safely, let's create a dedicated space. Navigate to your home directory (`cd ~`) and create a new directory called `playground`:

```
$ pwd
/home/your_username
$ mkdir playground
$ cd playground
$ pwd
/home/your_username/playground
```

Now you have a safe sandbox where you can experiment without affecting important system files or your personal documents. Let's get started!

Creating Empty Files

Sometimes you just need a file to exist, perhaps as a placeholder, before you put content into it, or maybe to update its timestamp. The command for this is touch.

If you provide touch with a filename that doesn't exist, it creates an empty file with that name.

```
$ ls -l
total 0
$ touch my_first_file.txt
$ ls -l
total 0
-rw-r--r-- 1 your_username users 0 Jul 23 14:10 my_first_file.txt
```

See? my_first_file.txt now exists, and ls -l shows its size is 0 bytes.

You can also create multiple files at once:

```
$ touch report.log draft_notes project_plan.doc
$ ls
draft_notes  my_first_file.txt  project_plan.doc  report.log
```

What if the file already exists? In that case, touch updates the file's **last modification timestamp** to the current time without changing its contents. This can be useful for various reasons, for example, signaling to build systems that a file needs recompiling, or simply marking when you last worked with it.

```
$ ls -l my_first_file.txt
-rw-r--r-- 1 your_username users 0 Jul 23 14:10 my_first_file.txt
$ # Wait a minute or two...
$ touch my_first_file.txt
$ ls -l my_first_file.txt
-rw-r--r-- 1 your_username users 0 Jul 23 14:12 my_first_file.txt
```

Notice how the timestamp updated. touch is a simple but handy utility.

Creating Directories

Just as you need files, you need folders, or **directories** as they're called in Linux, to organize them. The command to **make dir**ectories is `mkdir`.

Like `touch`, you provide `mkdir` with the name(s) of the directories you want to create.

```
$ pwd
/home/your_username/playground
$ mkdir TextFiles Spreadsheets Notes
$ ls -l
total 12
drwxr-xr-x 2 your_username users 4096 Jul 23 14:15 Notes
drwxr-xr-x 2 your_username users 4096 Jul 23 14:15 Spreadsheets
drwxr-xr-x 2 your_username users 4096 Jul 23 14:15 TextFiles
-rw-r--r-- 1 your_username users    0 Jul 23 14:12 draft_notes
-rw-r--r-- 1 your_username users    0 Jul 23 14:12 my_first_file.txt
-rw-r--r-- 1 your_username users    0 Jul 23 14:12 project_plan.doc
-rw-r--r-- 1 your_username users    0 Jul 23 14:10 report.log
```

You now have three new subdirectories inside `playground`. Remember the `d` at the beginning of the permissions string in `ls -l` indicates a directory.

What if you want to create nested directories, like `playground/Archive/2024/Reports`? If `Archive` or `2024` don't exist yet, a simple `mkdir Archive/2024/Reports` will fail.

```
$ mkdir Archive/2024/Reports
mkdir: cannot create directory 'Archive/2024/Reports': No such file or directory
```

To handle this, use the `-p` (parents) option. This tells `mkdir` to create any necessary parent directories along the way.

```
$ mkdir -p Archive/2024/Reports
$ ls
Archive   draft_notes         my_first_file.txt  report.log    TextFiles
Notes     project_plan.doc    Spreadsheets
$ ls Archive/
2024
$ ls Archive/2024/
Reports
```

Success! The -p option is very convenient for creating deeper directory structures quickly.

Copying Things

Now that you can create files and directories, you'll inevitably need to duplicate them. The command for this is cp, short for **copy**.

The basic syntax is:

```
cp [options] source destination
```

Copying Files

To copy a file, specify the source file and the destination filename or directory.

Let's copy my_first_file.txt to a new file called my_second_file.txt:

```
$ ls
Archive   draft_notes        my_first_file.txt  report.log     TextFiles
Notes     project_plan.doc   Spreadsheets
$ cp my_first_file.txt my_second_file.txt
$ ls
Archive        draft_notes        my_second_file.txt  report.log     TextFiles
Notes          my_first_file.txt  project_plan.doc    Spreadsheets
```

Now you have two identical (though empty, in this case) files.

You can also copy a file *into* a directory. If the destination is an existing directory, cp places a copy of the source file inside that directory, keeping the original filename.

```
$ cp report.log TextFiles/
$ ls TextFiles/
report.log
```

You can copy multiple files into a directory at once by listing all the source files before the destination directory:

```
$ cp draft_notes project_plan.doc TextFiles/
$ ls TextFiles/
draft_notes  project_plan.doc  report.log
```

What if the destination file already exists? By default, cp will silently overwrite it! This can be dangerous. To be prompted before overwriting, use the -i (interactive) option:

```
$ cp -i my_first_file.txt TextFiles/report.log
cp: overwrite 'TextFiles/report.log'? y  # Type 'y' and Enter to confirm
$ # Or type 'n' and Enter to cancel
```

Many Linux distributions actually set up an *alias* so that cp automatically behaves like cp -i. An alias is a shortcut or substitution for a command (we'll cover aliases in Chapter 8). This is a safety feature. If you ever *want* to force an overwrite without being prompted (use with caution!), you might need to use \cp to bypass the alias or use the -f (force) option, though -i is generally safer.

Copying Directories

If you try to copy a directory using cp like you copy a file, you'll get an error:

```
$ cp TextFiles/ CopiedTextFiles
cp: -r not specified; omitting directory 'TextFiles/'
```

The error message gives you the clue: to copy a directory and all its contents (including subdirectories), you need to use the -r or -R option, which stands for **recursive**.

```
$ cp -r TextFiles CopiedTextFiles
$ ls
Archive          CopiedTextFiles    my_first_file.txt    report.log
Notes            draft_notes        my_second_file.txt   Spreadsheets
TextFiles        project_plan.doc
$ ls CopiedTextFiles/
draft_notes  project_plan.doc  report.log
```

Now CopiedTextFiles is a complete duplicate of the TextFiles directory and its contents. The -r option is essential for working with directories.

A common and useful combination is cp -ar. The -a (archive) option is often used for backups. It implies -r (recursive) and also preserves permissions, ownership, timestamps, and symbolic links, making the copy as identical to the original as possible. We'll learn more about permissions and ownership in Chapter 5.

Moving and Renaming

Sometimes you don't want to copy; you want to **move** a file or directory to a different location, or simply rename it. The command for both these actions is `mv`, short for **move**. Its syntax is very similar to `cp`:

```
mv [options] source destination
```

Moving Files and Directories

If the destination is an existing directory, `mv` moves the source file or directory *into* that destination directory.

```
$ pwd
/home/your_username/playground
$ ls
Archive          CopiedTextFiles   my_first_file.txt   report.log
Notes            draft_notes       my_second_file.txt  Spreadsheets
TextFiles        project_plan.doc
$ mv my_second_file.txt Notes/  # Move file into Notes directory
$ mv Spreadsheets Archive/2024/ # Move directory into Archive/2024
$ ls
Archive          CopiedTextFiles   my_first_file.txt   report.log
Notes            draft_notes       project_plan.doc    TextFiles
$ ls Notes/
my_second_file.txt
$ ls Archive/2024/
Reports   Spreadsheets
```

Unlike `cp`, you don't need a special option like `-r` to move directories; `mv` handles both files and directories naturally.

Renaming Files and Directories

How do you rename something? You use `mv`! If the destination is a *new filename* (in the same directory) and not an existing directory name, `mv` renames the source file or directory.

```
$ ls Notes/
my_second_file.txt
$ mv Notes/my_second_file.txt Notes/important_notes.txt
$ ls Notes/
```

```
important_notes.txt
```

The file `my_second_file.txt` is now called `important_notes.txt`. You can rename directories the same way:

```
$ ls
Archive          CopiedTextFiles  my_first_file.txt  report.log
Notes            draft_notes      project_plan.doc   TextFiles
$ mv CopiedTextFiles TextFilesBackup
$ ls
Archive          Notes            my_first_file.txt  report.log
TextFilesBackup  draft_notes      project_plan.doc   TextFiles
```

Think of renaming as moving a file or directory to a new name *within the same location*.

Like `cp`, `mv` will overwrite existing files at the destination without warning by default. Use the `-i` (interactive) option to be prompted before overwriting:

```
$ touch file_A
$ touch file_B
$ mv -i file_A file_B
mv: overwrite 'file_B'?
```

Again, your distribution might have an alias for `mv` to include `-i` automatically. Use \ `mv` or `mv  -f` to force an overwrite if needed, but be careful!

Deleting Safely

Eventually, you'll need to clean up and remove files or directories you no longer need. Be extra cautious with these commands, as **deleted files in Linux are generally gone for good** – there's no standard "Recycle Bin" on the command line!

Removing Empty Directories

The safest deletion command is `rmdir`, which **removes dir**ectories. Crucially, `rmdir` only works on **empty** directories.

Let's try removing the `TextFiles` directory we created earlier (which is not empty):

```
$ rmdir TextFiles
rmdir: failed to remove 'TextFiles': Directory not empty
```

As expected, it fails. Let's create an empty one and remove it:

```
$ mkdir EmptyFolder
$ ls
Archive          Notes           my_first_file.txt  report.log
EmptyFolder      TextFilesBackup  draft_notes         project_plan.doc
TextFiles
$ rmdir EmptyFolder
$ ls
Archive          Notes           my_first_file.txt  report.log
TextFilesBackup  draft_notes     project_plan.doc   TextFiles
```

It worked because `EmptyFolder` contained nothing. `rmdir` is safe because it prevents you from accidentally deleting a directory that still has files inside.

Removing Files and Directories

The more powerful (and therefore more dangerous) command for removing files is rm, short for **remove**.

To remove a single file:

```
$ ls
Archive          Notes           my_first_file.txt  report.log
TextFilesBackup  draft_notes     project_plan.doc   TextFiles
$ rm draft_notes
$ ls
Archive          Notes           my_first_file.txt  report.log
TextFilesBackup  project_plan.doc TextFiles
```

To remove multiple files, list their names:

```
$ rm my_first_file.txt project_plan.doc report.log
$ ls
Archive  Notes  TextFiles  TextFilesBackup
```

Similar to cp and mv, rm often has an alias to include the -i (interactive) option, prompting you before deleting each file. This is highly recommended.

```
$ touch temp_file
$ rm temp_file # Assuming rm is aliased to rm -i
rm: remove regular empty file 'temp_file'? y
$ ls
```

To remove a directory and *all* its contents (files, subdirectories, everything inside), you need the -r (recursive) option. This is where you must be extremely careful.

```
$ ls TextFilesBackup/
draft_notes  project_plan.doc  report.log
$ rm -r TextFilesBackup/
$ ls
Archive  Notes  TextFiles
```

The TextFilesBackup directory and everything it contained are now gone.

A Word of Caution

You will often see the command rm -rf directory_name or rm -rf * used in examples online or by experienced users.

- -r: Recursive (delete directories and their contents).
- -f: Force (attempt to remove without prompting, ignore non-existent files, never prompt).

Combining these two options, rm -rf, tells the system to **forcefully delete the specified directory (or files) and everything inside it, recursively, without asking for any confirmation.**

This command is incredibly dangerous if misused! A small typo, like adding an extra space (rm -rf / mydirectory instead of rm -rf /mydirectory) or running it in the wrong directory (rm -rf * in / instead of ~/playground), could potentially **wipe out your entire system or all your personal files.**

Always double-check your pwd (current directory) and the target of your rm -rf command before pressing Enter. There is no undo. Using -i whenever possible is a much safer habit, especially when learning. Use rm -rf only when you are absolutely certain you know what you are doing and what you are deleting.

Using Wildcards for Bulk Operations

Typing out every single filename for cp, mv, or rm can be tedious if you have many files. The shell provides special characters called **wildcards** (or globbing patterns) that let you specify multiple files based on patterns in their names.

- ✱ (Asterisk): Matches **zero or more** characters. This is the most powerful and common wildcard.

  - ✱.txt: Matches all files ending with .txt.
  - report✱: Matches all files starting with report.
  - ✱data✱: Matches all files containing data anywhere in their name.
- ? (Question Mark): Matches exactly **one** character.

  - file?.log: Matches file1.log, fileA.log, but not file10.log or file.log.
  - ???: Matches any filename that is exactly three characters long.
- [] (Square Brackets): Matches exactly **one** character from the set specified within the brackets.

  - [abc].txt: Matches a.txt, b.txt, or c.txt.
  - [0-9].log: Matches 0.log, 1.log, ..., 9.log (using a range).
  - [a-zA-Z]✱.dat: Matches any file starting with an uppercase or lower-case letter and ending in .dat.
  - [!abc].txt or [^abc].txt: Matches any single character *except* a, b, or c followed by .txt.

Let's see some examples in our playground/TextFiles directory. First, let's create some sample files:

```
$ cd TextFiles/
$ touch report_jan.log report_feb.log draft_v1.txt draft_v2.txt summary.txt
$ ls
draft_notes       draft_v2.txt   report_feb.log  report.log  summary.txt
draft_v1.txt      project_plan.doc report_jan.log
```

Now, let's use wildcards:

```
$ # List all files ending in .log
$ ls *.log
report_feb.log  report_jan.log  report.log

$ # List all files starting with draft_
$ ls draft_*
draft_notes  draft_v1.txt  draft_v2.txt

$ # List files with 'v' followed by exactly one character, then .txt
$ ls draft_v?.txt
draft_v1.txt  draft_v2.txt
```

```
$ # Create a backup directory and copy all .log files into it
$ mkdir ../LogsBackup
$ cp *.log ../LogsBackup/
$ ls ../LogsBackup/
report_feb.log  report_jan.log  report.log

$ # Remove all files starting with draft_
$ rm -i draft_* # Use -i for safety!
rm: remove regular empty file 'draft_notes'? y
rm: remove regular empty file 'draft_v1.txt'? y
rm: remove regular empty file 'draft_v2.txt'? y
$ ls
project_plan.doc  report_feb.log  report_jan.log  report.log  summary.txt
```

Important: The shell expands the wildcards *before* the command runs. When you type cp *.log ../LogsBackup/, the shell first finds all matching filenames (report_feb.log, report_jan.log, report.log) and then effectively runs cp report_feb.log report_jan.log report.log ../LogsBackup/. This expansion happens first. Be careful when using wildcards with destructive commands like rm! Use ls with the wildcard pattern first to see what files *will* be matched before you actually delete them.

Finding Lost Items

Sometimes you know a file exists, but you've forgotten where you put it. Linux offers powerful tools to search the filesystem.

The Powerhouse

The find command is incredibly versatile (and can seem complex at first). It recursively searches directory trees for files matching specified criteria. The basic syntax is:

```
find [path...] [expression]
```

- [path...]: Where to start searching (e.g., /, ~, .). If omitted, it searches the current directory.
- [expression]: The criteria for matching files (e.g., by name, type, size, modification time).

Let's try some common uses:

- **Find by Name:** Use the -name option (case-sensitive) or -iname (case-insensitive). Wildcards can be used, but you **must quote them** to prevent the shell from expanding them *before* find runs.

```
$ # Find all files named 'report.log' starting from playground
$ find ~/playground -name report.log
/home/your_username/playground/LogsBackup/report.log
/home/your_username/playground/TextFiles/report.log

$ # Find all files ending in .log (case-insensitive) in current dir (.)
$ find . -iname '*.log'
./LogsBackup/report_feb.log
./LogsBackup/report_jan.log
./LogsBackup/report.log
./TextFiles/report_feb.log
./TextFiles/report_jan.log
./TextFiles/report.log
```

Remember the quotes around *.log*!*

- **Find by Type:** Use the -type option. Common types are f (regular file) and d (directory).

```
$ # Find all directories within playground
$ find ~/playground -type d
/home/your_username/playground
/home/your_username/playground/TextFiles
/home/your_username/playground/Notes
/home/your_username/playground/Archive
/home/your_username/playground/Archive/2024
/home/your_username/playground/Archive/2024/Reports
/home/your_username/playground/Archive/2024/Spreadsheets
/home/your_username/playground/LogsBackup
```

- **Combining Criteria:** You can combine tests. By default, they are joined by a logical AND.

```
$ # Find directories named 'Reports'
$ find ~/playground -type d -name Reports
/home/your_username/playground/Archive/2024/Reports
```

- **Executing Commands on Found Files:** The -exec option lets you run a command on each file found. {} is replaced by the filename, and the command must end with \;.

```
$ # Find all .log files in LogsBackup and run 'ls -l' on them
$ find ~/playground/LogsBackup -name '*.log' -exec ls -l {} \;
-rw-r--r-- 1 your_username users 0 Jul 23 14:45
/home/your_username/playground/LogsBackup/report_feb.log
-rw-r--r-- 1 your_username users 0 Jul 23 14:45
/home/your_username/playground/LogsBackup/report_jan.log
-rw-r--r-- 1 your_username users 0 Jul 23 14:10
/home/your_username/playground/LogsBackup/report.log
```

find has many, many more options (searching by size, time, permissions, etc.). Check man find when you need more advanced searching capabilities. It's a tool worth investing time in learning.

The Quick Search

Searching with find can be slow, especially if you're searching large parts of the filesystem, because it actively traverses the directories *at the time you run the command*.

An alternative is locate. This command searches a pre-built **database** of filenames on your system. Because it's just querying a database, locate is incredibly fast.

```
$ locate report.log
/home/your_username/playground/LogsBackup/report.log
/home/your_username/playground/TextFiles/report.log
/var/log/somelog/report.log  # Might find other files too!
```

The catch? The database might not be perfectly up-to-date. It's typically updated automatically on a regular schedule (e.g., once a day) by a command called updatedb. If you just created a file, locate might not find it immediately until the database is refreshed. You can usually run sudo updatedb manually to force an update (you might need sudo because the database is system-wide).

So, locate is great for quick searches when you know the filename (or part of it) and the file isn't brand new. Use find for more complex criteria or when you need real-time results.

Chapter Summary

You're now equipped with the fundamental toolkit for managing files and directories! We started by creating empty files with touch and directories with mkdir (using -p for convenience). You learned how to duplicate files and directories using cp (remembering -r for directories) and how to move or rename them with mv. We tackled deletion using the safe rmdir for empty directories and the powerful rm for files and populated directories (always being mindful of the -r and -f options and the extreme caution needed with rm -rf). We then unlocked the efficiency of wildcards (*, ?, []) to perform operations on multiple files matching specific patterns. Finally, you learned how to search for files across the system using the fast database-driven locate and the powerful, real-time searching capabilities of find.

You can now not only navigate the filesystem but also actively shape it. In the next chapter, we'll focus on how to actually *view* the contents of the files you've been creating and managing, using essential tools like cat, less, more, head, and tail.

4

Looking Inside Files

So far, you've become adept at navigating the filesystem (Chapter 2) and managing its contents – creating, copying, moving, and deleting files and directories (Chapter 3). But what about the actual *information* stored within those files? It's time to peek inside! Whether you need to quickly check a configuration setting, read a log message, or browse through a script you've written, knowing how to view file content without necessarily changing it is a fundamental skill. In this chapter, we'll explore the essential Linux commands designed specifically for displaying file contents in various ways, from showing the whole file at once to viewing just the beginning or end, or paging through large files conveniently. We'll also take our first tentative steps into the world of text editing.

Let's create a sample text file to work with. We'll use a command called echo along with output redirection (which we'll cover fully in Chapter 6) to quickly put some text into a file named planets.txt in your playground directory.

```
$ cd ~/playground
$ echo "Mercury" > planets.txt
$ echo "Venus" >> planets.txt
$ echo "Earth" >> planets.txt
$ echo "Mars" >> planets.txt
$ echo "Jupiter" >> planets.txt
$ echo "Saturn" >> planets.txt
$ echo "Uranus" >> planets.txt
$ echo "Neptune" >> planets.txt
```

```
$ # Maybe we should add Pluto for old times' sake?
$ echo "Pluto (Dwarf Planet)" >> planets.txt
```

Now we have a simple file containing a list of planets, ready for inspection.

Quick Peeks

The most straightforward command for displaying the *entire* content of a file (or multiple files) is cat, which stands for con**cat**enate. It reads the specified file(s) and prints their content directly to your terminal screen (standard output).

To view our planets.txt file:

```
$ cat planets.txt
Mercury
Venus
Earth
Mars
Jupiter
Saturn
Uranus
Neptune
Pluto (Dwarf Planet)
```

Simple! cat just dumps the whole file content out.

As its name suggests, cat can also concatenate (link together) multiple files. If you give it more than one filename, it displays them one after the other.

Let's create another small file:

```
$ echo "Our Moon" > moons.txt
$ echo "Phobos" >> moons.txt
$ echo "Deimos" >> moons.txt
```

Now, let's cat both files:

```
$ cat planets.txt moons.txt
Mercury
Venus
Earth
Mars
Jupiter
```

```
Saturn
Uranus
Neptune
Pluto (Dwarf Planet)
Our Moon
Phobos
Deimos
```

You can use this concatenation feature with redirection (>) to combine files:

```
$ cat planets.txt moons.txt > celestial_bodies.txt
$ cat celestial_bodies.txt
Mercury
Venus
Earth
Mars
Jupiter
Saturn
Uranus
Neptune
Pluto (Dwarf Planet)
Our Moon
Phobos
Deimos
```

A useful option for cat is -n, which numbers all output lines:

```
$ cat -n planets.txt
     1  Mercury
     2  Venus
     3  Earth
     4  Mars
     5  Jupiter
     6  Saturn
     7  Uranus
     8  Neptune
     9  Pluto (Dwarf Planet)
```

Potential Pitfall: cat is great for short files. However, if you use cat on a very long file (like a large log file or a lengthy program source code), it will dump the *entire* contents to your screen uncontrollably, potentially scrolling past the information you wanted to see faster than you can read it. For larger files, you'll want a pager.

Viewing Page by Page

When `cat` is too much because the file is too long, you need a **pager** – a program that displays text one screenful (or "page") at a time. The two classic pagers on Linux are `more` and `less`.

more

`more` is the original UNIX pager. It's simple: it displays the file content one screenful at a time. You press the `Spacebar` to advance to the next page and `q` to quit.

```
$ # Let's imagine celestial_bodies.txt was very long
$ more celestial_bodies.txt
Mercury
Venus
Earth
Mars
Jupiter
Saturn
Uranus
Neptune
Pluto (Dwarf Planet)
Our Moon
Phobos
Deimos
--More--(%)  # Press Spacebar to see more (if there was more) or q to quit
```

`more` is functional but quite basic. You generally can't easily scroll backward.

less

`less` was developed later as a significant improvement over `more`. Its name is a playful reference: "**less** is **more**". `less` allows you to scroll both forward *and backward*, search for text within the file, display line numbers, and much more, all without having to load the entire file into memory first (which makes it efficient for huge files). `less` **is the pager you should generally prefer.**

Let's view our file with `less`:

```
$ less celestial_bodies.txt
```

Your terminal screen will fill with the beginning of the file. You'll see the content, and usually a colon (:) or the filename at the bottom left, indicating `less` is active and waiting for your commands.

Navigating within `less`

Here are the essential commands for navigating within `less` (you don't type Enter after these):

- **Scrolling:**

  - `Spacebar` or `PageDown`: Scroll forward one screenful.
  - `b` or `PageUp`: Scroll backward one screenful.
  - `Down Arrow` or `j`: Scroll forward one line.
  - `Up Arrow` or `k`: Scroll backward one line.
  - `g`: Go to the beginning of the file.
  - `G`: Go to the end of the file.

- **Searching:**

  - `/pattern`: Type / followed by the text you want to search for, then press `Enter`. `less` will jump to the first occurrence *after* your current position.
  - `?pattern`: Type ? followed by the text, then press `Enter`. `less` will jump to the first occurrence *before* your current position.
  - `n`: Find the next occurrence of the last search pattern (in the same direction).
  - `N`: Find the Next occurrence of the last search pattern (in the opposite direction).

- **Other Useful Commands:**

  - `-N` (Option when starting): `less -N filename` displays line numbers.
  - `=` (While running): Shows your current position in the file (line number, percentage).
  - `h`: Displays a help screen summarizing commands.
  - `q`: Quit `less` and return to the shell prompt.

Let's try searching for "Mars":

```
$ less celestial_bodies.txt
Mercury
Venus
Earth
```

```
Mars          # <-- Cursor jumps here after search
Jupiter
...
/Mars         # <-- Type /Mars and press Enter at the bottom
```

Practice using less with different files (try /etc/services or a log file in /var/log if you have permission – be careful not to change anything!). Getting comfortable with less navigation is key to efficiently reading files on the command line.

Seeing the Beginning

Sometimes you don't need the whole file, just the first few lines. This is useful for checking the headers of a log file, the beginning of a script, or the first few entries in a data file. The command for this is head.

By default, head displays the first **10 lines** of a file.

```
$ head celestial_bodies.txt
Mercury
Venus
Earth
Mars
Jupiter
Saturn
Uranus
Neptune
Pluto (Dwarf Planet)
Our Moon
```

You can specify a different number of lines using the -n option, or more compactly, just a hyphen followed by the number.

```
$ # Show the first 3 lines
$ head -n 3 celestial_bodies.txt
Mercury
Venus
Earth

$ # Same thing, using the shorter syntax
$ head -3 celestial_bodies.txt
Mercury
Venus
```

head is simple and effective for grabbing the top portion of any text file.

Seeing the End

Conversely, you often want to see the *last* few lines of a file. This is incredibly common when checking log files, as the newest messages are usually appended to the end. The command for this is `tail`.

By default, `tail` displays the last **10 lines** of a file.

```
$ tail celestial_bodies.txt
Earth
Mars
Jupiter
Saturn
Uranus
Neptune
Pluto (Dwarf Planet)
Our Moon
Phobos
Deimos
```

Just like `head`, you can specify the number of lines to show using `-n` or the hyphen syntax:

```
$ # Show the last 4 lines
$ tail -n 4 celestial_bodies.txt
Pluto (Dwarf Planet)
Our Moon
Phobos
Deimos

$ # Same thing, shorter syntax
$ tail -4 celestial_bodies.txt
Pluto (Dwarf Planet)
Our Moon
Phobos
Deimos
```

Following File Changes

One of the most powerful features of `tail` is its ability to **follow** a file. Using the `-f` option, `tail` displays the last few lines (10 by default) and then waits. When new lines are added to the end of the file by some other process, `tail -f` automatically prints them to your screen in real-time.

This is invaluable for monitoring log files or the output of long-running processes. Imagine a web server writing access requests to `/var/log/nginx/access.log`. You could watch new requests come in live:

```
$ # Hypothetical example - you might need 'sudo' for system logs
$ tail -f /var/log/syslog
Jul 23 15:01:01 mypc CRON[12345]: (root) CMD (command run by cron)
Jul 23 15:01:10 mypc kernel: [HardwareEvent] Some message...
# <-- Cursor waits here. As new lines are added to syslog, they appear -->

# To stop tail -f, press Ctrl+C
```

To exit `tail -f`, you need to interrupt it by pressing `Ctrl+C`. This sends an interrupt signal that tells the `tail` process to stop. `tail -f` is a command you'll use frequently when troubleshooting or monitoring system activity.

A Gentle Introduction to Text Editing

The tools we've seen so far (`cat`, `less`, `head`, `tail`) are excellent for *viewing* files. But what if you need to *change* the content? Fix a typo in `planets.txt`? Modify a configuration file? Write a shell script (which we'll start doing later in the book)? For this, you need a **text editor**.

The command line offers several text editors, ranging from very simple to incredibly powerful (and complex). We won't dive deep into editing techniques here, as that's a vast topic, but let's introduce two common editors you're likely to encounter.

Getting Started with nano

For beginners, `nano` is often the most approachable command-line text editor. It's modeless, meaning you just type text directly, similar to simple graphical editors like Notepad or TextEdit. Common commands are displayed right at the bottom of the screen, usually using ^ to represent the `Ctrl` key.

To edit (or create) a file with nano:

```
$ nano planets.txt
```

You'll see the file content loaded into the editor window.

```
  GNU nano 6.2                    planets.txt
Mercury
Venus
Earth
Mars
Jupiter
Saturn
Uranus
Neptune
Pluto (Dwarf Planet)




^G Help      ^O Write Out ^R Read File ^Y Prev Page ^K Cut Text   ^C Cur Pos
^X Exit      ^J Justify   ^W Where Is  ^V Next Page ^U Uncut Text^T To Spell
```

- **Editing:** Just use your arrow keys to move the cursor and type as you normally would. Use Backspace or Delete to remove characters.
- **Saving:** Press Ctrl+O (Write Out). nano will ask you to confirm the filename to write to (usually defaulting to the current name). Press Enter to save.
- **Exiting:** Press Ctrl+X (Exit). If you haven't saved your changes, nano will ask if you want to save them before exiting (press Y for yes, N for no, or Ctrl+C to cancel exiting).
- **Cutting/Pasting:** Ctrl+K cuts the current line (or selected text). Ctrl+U pastes the last cut text.
- **Searching:** Ctrl+W (Where Is) lets you search for text.

nano is designed to be intuitive. Explore the commands listed at the bottom (^G for Help is useful!). It's a great editor to start with for quick edits.

A Glimpse into vim

You cannot talk about Linux text editors without mentioning vim (Vi IMproved), or its ancestor vi. vim is an extremely powerful, highly efficient editor favored by many experienced programmers and system administrators. It's almost guaranteed to be available on any Linux or UNIX-like system you encounter.

However, `vim` has a significantly steeper learning curve than `nano` because it is a **modal** editor. This means it operates in different modes, primarily:

- **Normal Mode:** The default mode when you start `vim`. Keystrokes here are interpreted as commands (e.g., `d` to delete, `y` to yank/copy, `p` to paste, `x` to delete character, arrow keys or `h`/`j`/`k`/`l` to navigate). You don't just type text in Normal mode.
- **Insert Mode:** Activated by pressing `i` (or `a`, `o`, etc.) in Normal mode. Now, keystrokes insert text into the file, similar to `nano` or graphical editors. You press the `Esc` key to return to Normal mode.
- **Command-Line Mode:** Accessed by pressing `:` in Normal mode. Allows you to enter commands like saving (`:w`), quitting (`:q`), saving and quitting (`:wq`), or quitting without saving (`:q!`). Press `Enter` to execute the command.

The modal nature makes `vim` incredibly efficient once learned, as you can perform complex edits without constantly reaching for the mouse or modifier keys. But it can be baffling for newcomers – the most common beginner problem is getting "stuck" in `vim`, often because they're in Normal mode trying to type text or in Insert mode trying to enter a command.

To edit with `vim`:

```
$ vim planets.txt
```

Remember:

1. You start in Normal mode.
2. Press `i` to enter Insert mode and type text.
3. Press `Esc` to go back to Normal mode.
4. In Normal mode, type `:wq` to save and quit, or `:q!` to quit without saving changes.

Mastering `vim` is a skill in itself, often requiring dedicated tutorials or books. We won't cover it extensively here, but it's essential to know it exists, understand its basic modal concept, and critically, know how to exit it (`Esc`, then `:q!` is the panic button!). If you plan to do serious development or system administration on Linux, learning `vim` is often a worthwhile investment.

Chapter Summary

In this chapter, we shifted focus from managing files to viewing their contents. You learned how to display entire files quickly using `cat` and recognized its limitations with large files. We explored the indispensable pager `less` (and its older sibling `more`), mastering its navigation and search commands for comfortably viewing long files page by page. You also learned how to peek at just the beginning of files with `head` and the end with `tail`. Crucially, you discovered the power of `tail -f` for monitoring files like logs in real-time. Finally, we took our first look at command-line text editing, introducing the user-friendly `nano` and the powerful, ubiquitous, but modal `vim`, giving you the basic tools to make changes when viewing isn't enough.

Now that you can navigate, manage, view, and even make basic edits to files, it's time to understand a critical aspect of Linux: users and permissions. Who owns these files? Who is allowed to read, write, or execute them? Understanding this is vital for security and collaboration. In the next chapter, we'll delve into users, groups, file ownership, and the permission system that controls access to everything on your Linux system.

5

Understanding Users and Permissions

You've learned to navigate the filesystem (Chapter 2), manage files and directories (Chapter 3), and view their contents (Chapter 4). Now, we need to address a fundamental concept that underpins everything you do in Linux: **permissions**. Linux is inherently a multi-user system, designed from the ground up for multiple people (or processes) to use the same computer simultaneously without interfering with each other or accessing things they shouldn't. This is achieved through a system of users, groups, and permissions assigned to every file and directory. Understanding this system is not just about security; it's essential for collaboration, software installation, and ensuring your system runs smoothly. This chapter unlocks the "who," "what," and "how" of file access.

Who Are You?

First things first, let's figure out who the system thinks *you* are right now. There are two primary commands for this:

whoami

This command does exactly what it says: it prints the username you are currently logged in as.

```
$ whoami
jane
```

Simple and direct. It confirms your current user identity.

id

The `id` command gives you a more detailed picture of your identity, including your username, your unique numerical **User ID (UID)**, your primary **Group ID (GID)**, and a list of all the **groups** you belong to.

```
$ id
uid=1001(jane) gid=1001(jane) groups=1001(jane),10(wheel),998(docker)
```

Let's break this down:

- `uid=1001(jane)`: Your username is `jane`, and the system internally identifies you with the number `1001`. Every user has a unique UID. The root user, the superuser with all privileges, traditionally has UID `0`.
- `gid=1001(jane)`: Your primary group is also named `jane` (this is common on many modern distributions) and has the GID `1001`. When you create a new file, it typically belongs to your UID and this primary GID by default.
- `groups=1001(jane),10(wheel),998(docker)`: This lists all the groups you are a member of, including your primary group. Group membership grants you access privileges associated with that group. In this example, `jane` is also part of the `wheel` group (often used to control who can use `sudo`, as we'll see later) and the `docker` group (likely granting permissions to interact with Docker containers).

Every user and group on a Linux system has both a name (like `jane` or `wheel`) and a corresponding unique number (UID or GID). While you usually interact with the names, the kernel primarily works with the numbers internally.

Who Else Is Here?

Since Linux is multi-user, you might want to see who else is currently logged into the system.

who

The who command provides a simple list of users currently logged in, showing their username, the terminal they are connected from, and the time they logged in.

```
$ who
jane      tty1       2024-07-23 09:15 (:0)
peter     pts/0      2024-07-23 14:50 (192.168.1.105)
root      pts/1      2024-07-23 15:01 (server.local)
```

This shows jane logged in locally on a virtual console (tty1), peter logged in remotely via SSH (indicated by pts/0 and an IP address), and root also logged in remotely. pts stands for pseudo-terminal slave, typically used for remote connections or terminal emulator windows.

w

The w command gives you more information than who. It shows who is logged in, but also adds details like their **idle time**, how much CPU time they've used recently (JCPU, PCPU), and the **current command** they are running.

```
$ w
 15:10:30 up 5:55,  3 users,  load average: 0.05, 0.15, 0.11
USER     TTY        FROM             LOGIN@   IDLE   JCPU   PCPU WHAT
jane     tty1       :0               09:15    5:55m  1.20s  0.15s
/usr/libexec/gsd-xsettings
peter    pts/0      192.168.1.105    14:50    3.00s  0.05s  0.01s -bash
root     pts/1      server.local     15:01    9:20   0.02s  0.02s -bash
```

The first line gives system uptime, number of users, and load averages (a measure of system activity). The subsequent lines show details for each user. Notice the IDLE column (how long since they last typed anything) and the WHAT column showing their current activity. w is great for getting a quick snapshot of system usage and who's doing what.

Users vs. Groups

We saw users and groups in the `id` output. Let's solidify this concept.

- **User:** Represents an individual account that can log in, own files, and run processes. Each user has a unique UID. Think of this as your personal employee ID badge.
- **Group:** A collection of users. Groups are used to manage permissions for multiple users simultaneously. A user can belong to multiple groups. Think of groups like departments in a company (Sales, Engineering, Marketing).

Why have groups? Imagine a project directory containing files that several team members need to access and modify. Instead of granting permissions to each user individually, you could:

1. Create a group (e.g., `project_alpha_team`).
2. Add all the relevant team members to this group.
3. Set the permissions on the project directory so that members of the `project_alpha_team` group can read and write files within it.

Now, if a new member joins the team, you only need to add them to the group, and they instantly get the necessary access. If someone leaves, removing them from the group revokes their access to the shared files. It simplifies administration immensely compared to managing permissions per user.

Every user has a **primary group** (the one shown by `id`'s `gid=`). When you create a file, it usually gets assigned to your user and your primary group. You also belong to **supplementary groups** (listed in the `groups=` part of `id`), which grant you additional privileges based on those group memberships.

File Ownership

Every file and directory in Linux has exactly one **owner** (a user) and one **group** associated with it. These determine the first two levels of permission checking.

Let's revisit the `ls -l` output from Chapter 3, focusing on the owner and group columns (columns 3 and 4):

```
$ ls -l ~/playground/planets.txt
-rw-r--r-- 1 jane jane 114 Jul 23 14:05 /home/jane/playground/planets.txt
#          ^ ^^^^ ^^^^
#            |  |    |
```

```
# Permissions |    Group (jane)
#           Owner (jane)
```

In this case, the file `planets.txt` is owned by the user `jane` and belongs to the group `jane`.

Sometimes, you need to change the owner or the group of a file or directory. For example, if a file was created by the wrong user, or if you want to assign a project file to a specific project group. **Important:** You generally need to be the **root user** (or use sudo, discussed later) to change the ownership of a file you don't already own. You can usually change the group of a file you own to any group you are a member of.

Changing Ownership

The `chown` (**ch**ange **own**er) command changes the user and/or group ownership of a file or directory.

Syntax:

```
chown [options] NEW_OWNER[:NEW_GROUP] file_or_directory...
```

- `NEW_OWNER`: The username (or UID) of the new owner.
- `NEW_GROUP` (Optional): If preceded by a colon (`:`), specifies the new group as well. If the colon is present but no group name follows (e.g., `chown jane:`), the file's group is changed to the new owner's primary group.

Examples:

Let's assume we have another user `peter` and a group `science_proj`.

```
$ # Create a file as jane
$ touch project_data.dat
$ ls -l project_data.dat
-rw-r--r-- 1 jane jane 0 Jul 23 15:30 project_data.dat

$ # Change owner to peter (requires root/sudo)
$ sudo chown peter project_data.dat
$ ls -l project_data.dat
-rw-r--r-- 1 peter jane 0 Jul 23 15:30 project_data.dat

$ # Change owner to peter AND group to science_proj (requires root/sudo)
$ sudo chown peter:science_proj project_data.dat
$ ls -l project_data.dat
```

```
-rw-r--r-- 1 peter science_proj 0 Jul 23 15:30 project_data.dat

$ # Change group back to jane's primary group (requires root/sudo)
$ sudo chown peter: project_data.dat
$ ls -l project_data.dat
-rw-r--r-- 1 peter jane 0 Jul 23 15:30 project_data.dat
```

To change ownership recursively for a directory and all its contents, use the -R option:

```
$ mkdir ProjectX
$ touch ProjectX/file1 ProjectX/file2
$ # Change ownership of directory and contents (requires root/sudo)
$ sudo chown -R peter:science_proj ProjectX/
$ ls -lR ProjectX/ # Use -R with ls to see inside recursively
ProjectX/:
total 0
-rw-r--r-- 1 peter science_proj 0 Jul 23 15:35 file1
-rw-r--r-- 1 peter science_proj 0 Jul 23 15:35 file2
```

Changing Group Ownership

If you only want to change the group ownership, you can use the chgrp (**change group**) command. The syntax is simpler:

```
chgrp [options] NEW_GROUP file_or_directory...
```

You generally need to be the owner of the file *and* a member of the NEW_GROUP to use chgrp without sudo. Otherwise, you'll likely need sudo.

```
$ # Assuming 'jane' owns project_data.dat and is a member of 'science_proj'
$ ls -l project_data.dat
-rw-r--r-- 1 jane jane 0 Jul 23 15:30 project_data.dat
$ chgrp science_proj project_data.dat
$ ls -l project_data.dat
-rw-r--r-- 1 jane science_proj 0 Jul 23 15:30 project_data.dat

$ # Change group recursively for a directory
$ sudo chgrp -R science_proj ProjectX/ # Need sudo if jane doesn't own it
$ ls -lR ProjectX/
ProjectX/:
total 0
-rw-r--r-- 1 peter science_proj 0 Jul 23 15:35 file1
-rw-r--r-- 1 peter science_proj 0 Jul 23 15:35 file2
```

While `chown user:group file` can do what `chgrp` does, `chgrp` exists as a dedicated command for just changing the group.

File Permissions

We've seen the ownership, now let's tackle the first part of the `ls -l` output: the permissions string like `-rw-r--r--`. This string defines who can do what with the file or directory.

There are three basic permission types:

- **Read (r):**
    - For files: Allows viewing the contents of the file (e.g., using `cat`, `less`).
    - For directories: Allows listing the names of the items *inside* the directory (e.g., using `ls`).
- **Write (w):**
    - For files: Allows modifying or deleting the *content* of the file (e.g., editing with `nano`, overwriting with `>`). Note: Deleting the file *itself* often depends on the permissions of the *directory* it's in.
    - For directories: Allows creating new files/subdirectories, deleting files/subdirectories, or renaming files/subdirectories *within* that directory (regardless of the permissions on the files themselves!). This is a crucial distinction. Write permission on a directory is powerful.
- **Execute (x):**
    - For files: Allows running the file as a program or script (if it's executable).
    - For directories: Allows **entering** the directory (e.g., using `cd`) and accessing files/subdirectories within it (provided you also have appropriate permissions on the items inside). You need execute permission on a directory to `cd` into it or access anything inside it, even if you can list its contents (read permission).

These three permissions (r, w, x) are defined for three distinct categories of users:

1. **User (u):** The owner of the file.
2. **Group (g):** Members of the group the file belongs to.
3. **Others (o):** Everyone else on the system (not the owner and not in the group).

Decoding Permissions (`ls -l` revisited)

Let's look at that string again: `drwxr-xr-x`

```
d | rwx | r-x | r-x
^ |  ^^^ |  ^^^ |  ^^^
| |  |    |     |
| |  |    |     +-- Others Permissions (Read, Execute)
| |  |    +-------- Group Permissions (Read, Execute)
| |  +------------- User (Owner) Permissions (Read, Write, Execute)
| +---------------- File Type (d=directory, -=file, l=link, etc.)
```

- **Type:** The first character (d) tells us it's a directory.
- **User/Owner:** The next three characters (rwx) mean the owner has Read, Write, and Execute permissions.
- **Group:** The next three (r-x) mean members of the group have Read and Execute permissions, but *not* Write (indicated by the hyphen -).
- **Others:** The final three (r-x) mean everyone else also has Read and Execute permissions, but not Write.

Here are some common examples:

- -rw-r--r--: A regular file (-) that the owner can read and write (rw-), while the group and others can only read (r--). Typical for data files or documents.
- -rwxr-xr-x: A regular file (-) that the owner can read, write, and execute (rwx), while the group and others can read and execute (r-x). Typical for executable programs or scripts shared with others.
- drwxr-x---: A directory (d) that the owner can list, enter, create/delete/ rename within (rwx). Group members can list and enter (r-x). Others have no permissions at all (---). Useful for semi-private project directories.

Directory Permissions Summary

Understanding directory permissions is key, as they control access to the files within them.

Permission	Allows you to...	Needed for commands like...
Read (r)	List the names of files/subdirs inside (e.g., ls)	ls (just names)
Write (w)	Create, delete, rename files/subdirs inside	touch, mkdir, rm, mv (within the dir)
Execute (x)	Enter the directory (cd), access items inside	cd, ls -l (to get details), cat file_inside

Important Combination: To read a file inside a directory, you need **Execute (x)** permission on the directory itself *plus* **Read (r)** permission on the file. To list the detailed contents using `ls -l`, you need **Read (r)** and **Execute (x)** permissions on the direct-ory.

Changing Permissions

Now, how do you change these permissions? The command is `chmod` (**change mode**). There are two main ways to specify the permissions you want to set: **Symbolic Mode** and **Octal Mode**.

Symbolic Mode (u, g, o, a, +, −, =)

Symbolic mode is generally easier to understand and read. You specify *who* (u, g, o, or a for all), *what operation* (+ to add, − to remove, = to set exactly), and *which permissions* (r, w, x).

Syntax:

```
chmod [who][operator][permissions] file_or_directory...
```

- **Who:**
    - u: User (owner)
    - g: Group
    - o: Others
    - a: All (equivalent to ugo) - This is the default if omitted.
- **Operator:**
    - +: Add the specified permission(s).
    - −: Remove the specified permission(s).
    - =: Set the permissions *exactly* as specified (removes any not listed).
- **Permissions:**
    - r: Read
    - w: Write
    - x: Execute

Examples:

Let's create a test file and script:

```
$ touch mydata.txt
$ echo '#!/bin/bash' > myscript.sh
$ echo 'echo "Hello from script!"' >> myscript.sh
```

```
$ ls -l
total 8
-rw-r--r-- 1 jane jane   0 Jul 23 16:00 mydata.txt
-rw-r--r-- 1 jane jane  39 Jul 23 16:01 myscript.sh
```

- **Make the script executable by the owner:**

```
$ chmod u+x myscript.sh
$ ls -l myscript.sh
-rwxr--r-- 1 jane jane 39 Jul 23 16:01 myscript.sh
$ ./myscript.sh # Now we can run it
Hello from script!
```

- **Remove write permission for the group and others on the data file:**

```
$ chmod go-w mydata.txt
$ ls -l mydata.txt
-rw-r--r-- 1 jane jane 0 Jul 23 16:00 mydata.txt # No change visible yet
if they didn't have w
$ # Let's make it world-writable first, then remove
$ chmod a+w mydata.txt
$ ls -l mydata.txt
-rw-rw-rw- 1 jane jane 0 Jul 23 16:00 mydata.txt
$ chmod go-w mydata.txt
$ ls -l mydata.txt
-rw-r----- 1 jane jane 0 Jul 23 16:00 mydata.txt # Now g and o are not
writable
```

- **Allow everyone to read the script, but only the owner to write/execute:**

```
$ chmod u=rwx,go=r myscript.sh # Set permissions exactly
$ ls -l myscript.sh
-rwxr--r-- 1 jane jane 39 Jul 23 16:01 myscript.sh
```

- **Make a directory accessible only by the owner:**

```
$ mkdir PrivateStuff
$ chmod u=rwx,go= PrivateStuff # '=PrivateStuff' removes all perms for g
and o
$ ls -ld PrivateStuff # Use -d to list directory itself, not contents
drwx------ 2 jane jane 4096 Jul 23 16:05 PrivateStuff
```

You can combine multiple specifications separated by commas (e.g., chmod u+x,g-w file). Symbolic mode is descriptive and good for making specific adjustments.

Octal (Numeric) Mode

Octal mode represents each set of permissions (user, group, others) as a single digit, derived by summing the values for each permission granted:

- Read (r) = **4**
- Write (w) = **2**
- Execute (x) = **1**
- No permission (-) = **0**

You combine these to get the value for each triplet:

- rwx = 4 + 2 + 1 = **7**
- rw- = 4 + 2 + 0 = **6**
- r-x = 4 + 0 + 1 = **5**
- r-- = 4 + 0 + 0 = **4**
- -wx = 0 + 2 + 1 = **3** (Less common)
- -w- = 0 + 2 + 0 = **2** (Less common)
- --x = 0 + 0 + 1 = **1**
- --- = 0 + 0 + 0 = **0**

You then use a three-digit number to represent the permissions for user, group, and others, respectively.

Syntax:

```
chmod [options] OCTAL_MODE file_or_directory...
```

Examples:

Using our mydata.txt and myscript.sh:

- **Set typical permissions for a script (owner: rwx, group: r-x, others: r-x):** rwx r-x r-x -> 7 5 5

```
$ chmod 755 myscript.sh
$ ls -l myscript.sh
-rwxr-xr-x 1 jane jane 39 Jul 23 16:01 myscript.sh
```

- Set typical permissions for a private data file (owner: rw-, group: r--, others: ---): rw- r-- --- -> 6 4 0

```
$ chmod 640 mydata.txt
$ ls -l mydata.txt
-rw-r----- 1 jane jane 0 Jul 23 16:00 mydata.txt
```

- Set typical permissions for a public data file (owner: rw-, group: r--, others: r--): rw- r-- r-- -> 6 4 4

```
$ chmod 644 mydata.txt
$ ls -l mydata.txt
-rw-r--r-- 1 jane jane 0 Jul 23 16:00 mydata.txt
```

- Set permissions for a private directory (owner: rwx, group: ---, others: ---): rwx --- --- -> 7 0 0

```
$ chmod 700 PrivateStuff/
$ ls -ld PrivateStuff/
drwx------ 2 jane jane 4096 Jul 23 16:05 PrivateStuff
```

Octal mode is concise and widely used, especially in documentation and scripts. It sets the permissions absolutely. However, it's less intuitive than symbolic mode initially, and it's easier to make mistakes if you miscalculate the numbers. Pick the mode that feels more comfortable, but be familiar with both as you'll encounter them frequently.

Remember, you can use the -R option with chmod to change permissions recursively on directories and their contents, just like with chown and chgrp.

Running Commands as Superuser

Throughout the examples for chown, chgrp, and sometimes even chmod or updatedb, we occasionally needed to use the sudo command. What is it, and why do we need it?

Linux operates on the principle of **least privilege**. This means user accounts normally have limited permissions – just enough to do their everyday work, but not enough to modify critical system files or affect other users directly. This prevents accidental damage and enhances security.

However, sometimes you *need* elevated privileges, typically those of the **root** user (UID 0), who has unlimited power over the system. This is necessary for tasks like installing software, changing system-wide configurations, managing hardware, or changing ownership of files you don't own.

Instead of logging in directly as root (which is generally discouraged for routine work because it's too easy to make catastrophic mistakes), most modern distributions use the sudo command.

sudo stands for "superuser **do**" (or sometimes "substitute user do"). It allows a permitted user to execute a *single* command **as the root user** (or another specified user).

How it works:

1. You preface the command you need to run with elevated privileges with sudo:

   ```
   $ sudo some_command arguments
   ```

2. sudo checks a configuration file (typically /etc/sudoers) to see if *your* user account is allowed to run *that specific command* (or any command) as root.
3. If you are permitted, sudo will usually prompt you for **your own user password** (not the root password) to verify your identity.

   ```
   [sudo] password for jane: ******
   ```

   Note: Often, no stars or feedback appear as you type your password.
4. If the password is correct and you have permission, sudo executes the command (some_command arguments) with root privileges.
5. For a short period (often 5-15 minutes), sudo might remember that you authenticated, allowing you to run subsequent sudo commands without re-entering your password.

Analogy: Think of your regular user account as having the key to your own office. The root account has the master key to the entire building. Using sudo is like going to the security desk (the /etc/sudoers file), proving your identity (your password), and asking the guard (the sudo program) to briefly unlock a specific restricted door for you using the master key, but only if you're on the approved list. You don't get to keep the master key yourself.

When to use sudo:

- Installing or removing system-wide software (e.g., `sudo apt install package`, `sudo dnf remove package`).
- Editing system configuration files (e.g., `sudo nano /etc/fstab`).
- Managing services (e.g., `sudo systemctl start nginx`).
- Changing ownership or permissions on files you don't own (e.g., `sudo chown root:root /etc/myconfig`).
- Running commands that require low-level hardware access.

When NOT to use sudo:

- Do **not** use sudo for everyday tasks like navigating directories (cd), listing files (ls), viewing files (cat, less), copying/moving your own files (cp, mv), or running regular applications like a web browser or text editor on your own documents. Using sudo unnecessarily increases the risk of accidental damage.

Get into the habit of running commands as your normal user first. If you get a "Permission denied" error and you know you need elevated privileges for that specific task, *then* try it again with sudo.

Chapter Summary

This chapter was crucial for understanding how Linux manages access control. You learned how to identify yourself (whoami, id) and see who else is using the system (who, w). We demystified the core concepts of **users** and **groups**, recognizing their role in organizing permissions. We revisited the ls -l output to understand **file ownership** (owner and group) and learned how to change it using chown and chgrp. The heart of the chapter was exploring the three basic **permissions** – Read (r), Write (w), and Execute (x) – and how they apply differently to files and directories for the User, Group, and Others categories. You gained the power to modify these permissions using chmod in both the descriptive **symbolic mode** and the concise **octal mode**. Finally, we addressed the necessity of elevated privileges for certain tasks and learned how to use the sudo command safely and effectively to run commands as the superuser without compromising the principle of least privilege.

With a solid grasp of users, groups, and permissions, you now understand the fundamental security and organizational model of the Linux filesystem. You know who can access what and how to control that access. This knowledge paves the way for the next part of our journey, where we start leveraging the shell's power more directly. In Chapter 6, we'll explore how to redirect the flow of information between commands and files using input/output redirection and pipes – essential techniques for building powerful command-line workflows.

6

Redirecting Input and Output

We've journeyed through the filesystem, learned to manage files, and deciphered the crucial concepts of users and permissions in Chapter 5. You're getting comfortable issuing commands. But so far, most commands have simply taken input from your keyboard and displayed their output directly onto your terminal screen. What if you want to save that output to a file? Or use the output of one command as the input for another? This is where the real power of the Linux command line starts to shine – through **redirection** and **pipes**. These mechanisms let you control the flow of data, connecting commands and files together like building blocks to perform complex tasks with elegant simplicity. Get ready to become a data plumber on the command line!

The Three Standard Streams

Before we can redirect data, we need to understand where it usually comes from and goes. When a command runs, Linux automatically provides it with three standard communication channels, often called **streams**:

1. **Standard Input (stdin):** This is where a command normally *reads* its input from. By default, stdin is connected to your **keyboard**. When a command

waits for you to type something (like the `cat` command run without argu-ments), it's reading from `stdin`. Internally, it's represented by **file descriptor 0**.

2. **Standard Output (stdout):** This is where a command normally *writes* its suc-cessful output or results to. By default, `stdout` is connected to your **terminal screen**. When `ls` shows you a list of files or `date` prints the time, that's going to `stdout`. Internally, it's represented by **file descriptor 1**.

3. **Standard Error (stderr):** This is where a command normally writes its *error messages* or diagnostic output to. By default, `stderr` is *also* connected to your **terminal screen**. This ensures you see error messages even if you redirect the normal output elsewhere. Internally, it's represented by **file descriptor 2**.

Think of a command as a small workshop. `stdin` (0) is the "**In**" tray, where raw mater-ials (data) arrive from the keyboard. `stdout` (1) is the "**Out**" tray for finished goods (successful results) heading to the display screen. `stderr` (2) is the "**Scrap Bin**", also emptying onto the display screen, where error messages or rejected parts end up.

Knowing these three streams exist (and their corresponding numbers 0, 1, and 2) is key to understanding redirection.

Sending Output Elsewhere

What if you don't want the command's output cluttering your screen? What if you want to save it to a file for later analysis or use? This is precisely what output redirec-tion is for.

The > (greater-than symbol) operator redirects **standard output (stdout)** to a file.

Syntax:

```
command > output_file.txt
```

Let's try it. Instead of just listing files to the screen, let's save the detailed listing of our `playground` directory to a file:

```
$ pwd
/home/jane/playground
$ ls -l
total 20
drwx------ 2 jane jane 4096 Jul 23 16:05 Archive
drwxr-xr-x 2 jane science_proj 4096 Jul 23 15:35 LogsBackup
```

```
-rw-r--r-- 1 jane jane    0 Jul 23 16:00 mydata.txt
-rwxr-xr-x 1 jane jane   39 Jul 23 16:01 myscript.sh
drwxr-xr-x 2 jane jane 4096 Jul 23 16:05 Notes
drwx------ 2 jane jane 4096 Jul 23 16:05 PrivateStuff
drwxr-xr-x 2 jane science_proj 4096 Jul 23 15:35 TextFiles
$ ls -l > playground_contents.txt
$ # Notice: No output appeared on the screen!
$ ls -l playground_contents.txt # Check if the file was created
-rw-r--r-- 1 jane jane 349 Jul 23 16:45 playground_contents.txt
$ cat playground_contents.txt # View the file's content
total 20
drwx------ 2 jane jane 4096 Jul 23 16:05 Archive
drwxr-xr-x 2 jane science_proj 4096 Jul 23 15:35 LogsBackup
-rw-r--r-- 1 jane jane    0 Jul 23 16:00 mydata.txt
-rwxr-xr-x 1 jane jane   39 Jul 23 16:01 myscript.sh
drwxr-xr-x 2 jane jane 4096 Jul 23 16:05 Notes
drwx------ 2 jane jane 4096 Jul 23 16:05 PrivateStuff
drwxr-xr-x 2 jane science_proj 4096 Jul 23 15:35 TextFiles
```

The output of ls -l, which normally goes to stdout (the screen), was redirected by >
into the file playground_contents.txt. If the file didn't exist, it was created.

Important Pitfall: If the output file *already exists*, the > operator will **overwrite** its contents without warning!

```
$ echo "Original content" > important_data.txt
$ cat important_data.txt
Original content
$ date > important_data.txt # Overwrite the file with the date
$ cat important_data.txt
Tue Jul 23 16:50:15 EDT 2024
```

The original content is gone! Be very careful when using >. (Some shells allow you to
set an option like set -o noclobber to prevent accidental overwrites with >, but it's
not the default behavior).

Redirecting Standard Error (stderr)

What about error messages? The > operator only redirects stdout (file descriptor 1).
Error messages (stderr, file descriptor 2) will still appear on your screen. Sometimes
this is what you want, but other times you might want to capture errors separately.

To redirect stderr, you specify its file descriptor number (2) before the > symbol.

```
$ find /etc -name shadow # This likely causes permission errors
find: '/etc/cups/ssl': Permission denied
find: '/etc/polkit-1/rules.d': Permission denied
find: '/etc/audit': Permission denied
/etc/shadow
find: '/etc/ssl/private': Permission denied
... # More permission errors and maybe the actual file

$ # Redirect only stderr (2) to a file
$ find /etc -name shadow 2> find_errors.log
/etc/shadow # Normal output (stdout) still goes to the screen

$ # Now check the error file
$ cat find_errors.log
find: '/etc/cups/ssl': Permission denied
find: '/etc/polkit-1/rules.d': Permission denied
find: '/etc/audit': Permission denied
find: '/etc/ssl/private': Permission denied
...
```

Now the errors are neatly saved in find_errors.log, while the successful result /
etc/shadow (if found and accessible) still printed to the screen.

Redirecting Both stdout and stderr

What if you want *everything* – normal output and errors – saved to the same file?
There are two common ways to do this:

1. **The &> syntax (Bash/Zsh):** This is a convenient shorthand to redirect both
   stdout and stderr.

   ```
   $ find /etc -name shadow &> all_output.log
   $ # No output or errors on screen
   $ cat all_output.log
   find: '/etc/cups/ssl': Permission denied
   find: '/etc/polkit-1/rules.d': Permission denied
   find: '/etc/audit': Permission denied
   /etc/shadow
   find: '/etc/ssl/private': Permission denied
   ...
   ```

2. **The traditional > file 2>&1 syntax:** This is slightly more complex but works
   in more shells (POSIX standard). Let's break it down:

- > `all_output.log`: Redirects `stdout` (file descriptor 1) to `all_output.log`.
- `2>&1`: Redirects `stderr` (file descriptor 2) to the *current location* of `stdout` (file descriptor 1). Since `stdout` is already pointing to the file `all_output.log`, `stderr` gets sent there too. The order matters! `2>&1 > file` would not work the same way.

```
$ find /etc -name shadow > all_output_v2.log 2>&1
$ # No output or errors on screen
$ cat all_output_v2.log # Contains both stdout and stderr
find: '/etc/cups/ssl': Permission denied
find: '/etc/polkit-1/rules.d': Permission denied
find: '/etc/audit': Permission denied
/etc/shadow
find: '/etc/ssl/private': Permission denied
...
```

Both `&>` and `> file 2>&1` achieve the same goal of capturing all output. The first is often preferred for its brevity in shells that support it.

Appending Output

We saw that > overwrites existing files. What if you want to *add* output to the end of a file without erasing its current content? Use the **append** operator >> (two greater-than symbols).

If the file doesn't exist, >> creates it (just like >). If the file *does* exist, new output is added to the end.

Let's create a simple log file:

```
$ date > activity.log
$ cat activity.log
Tue Jul 23 17:05:10 EDT 2024

$ # Wait a few seconds... then append
$ whoami >> activity.log
$ cat activity.log
Tue Jul 23 17:05:10 EDT 2024
jane

$ # Append again
$ pwd >> activity.log
```

```
$ cat activity.log
Tue Jul 23 17:05:10 EDT 2024
jane
/home/jane/playground
```

Each command's output was appended as a new line (or lines) to `activity.log`. This is perfect for creating logs or accumulating results over time.

You can also append `stderr` using `2>>`:

```
$ # Run our find command again, appending errors to the previous log
$ find /etc -name hosts 2>> find_errors.log
/etc/hosts
/etc/avahi/hosts
$ cat find_errors.log # Shows old errors plus new ones
find: '/etc/cups/ssl': Permission denied
... (old errors) ...
find: '/etc/cups/ssl': Permission denied # Added by the second find run
find: '/etc/polkit-1/rules.d': Permission denied
find: '/etc/audit/rules.d': Permission denied
find: '/etc/ssl/private': Permission denied
```

And you can append both `stdout` and `stderr` using `&>>` (Bash/Zsh) or `>> file 2>&1`:

```
$ # Append all output from 'date' command
$ date &>> combined_log.log

$ # Append all output from 'find' command
$ find /etc -name fstab >> combined_log.log 2>&1
$ cat combined_log.log # Contains output/errors from both commands
Tue Jul 23 17:15:01 EDT 2024
find: '/etc/cups/ssl': Permission denied
find: '/etc/polkit-1/rules.d': Permission denied
/etc/fstab
find: '/etc/audit/rules.d': Permission denied
find: '/etc/ssl/private': Permission denied
```

Use `>>` when you want to preserve existing content and add to it.

Taking Input from Files

Just as you can redirect output *to* a file, you can redirect input *from* a file. The < (less-than symbol) operator redirects **standard input (stdin)**, telling a command to read its input from a specified file instead of the keyboard.

Syntax:

```
command < input_file.txt
```

Many commands can take a filename as an argument (like `cat planets.txt`). However, some commands are designed specifically to read from `stdin`. Input redirection is essential for feeding data to such commands. Common examples include `sort`, `uniq`, `wc`, `tr`, `grep` (when no file arguments are given), and `cat` (when run without arguments).

Let's revisit our `planets.txt` file from Chapter 4. We can count the lines, words, and characters using `wc` (word count):

```
$ # Method 1: Giving filename as argument
$ wc planets.txt
  9  11 114 planets.txt # Output includes filename

$ # Method 2: Redirecting stdin from the file
$ wc < planets.txt
  9  11 114 # Output does NOT include filename
```

Both give the same counts (9 lines, 11 words, 114 characters), but notice the subtle difference: when reading from `stdin` via <, `wc` doesn't know the original filename, so it doesn't print it.

Let's try sorting the planets:

```
$ sort < planets.txt
Earth
Jupiter
Mars
Mercury
Neptune
Pluto (Dwarf Planet)
Saturn
Uranus
Venus
```

The `sort` command read the lines from `planets.txt` (because we redirected `stdin`) and printed the sorted lines to its `stdout` (the screen).

Input redirection is less frequently typed interactively than output redirection but is extremely important when writing scripts that process data stored in files.

Here Documents (<<) and Here Strings (<<<)

Sometimes, the input you want to provide to a command isn't stored in a separate file, but you want to include it directly in your command line or script. This is where Here Documents and Here Strings come in handy.

Here Documents (<<)

A **Here Document** allows you to embed multi-line input for a command directly following the command itself. You specify a delimiter word, and the shell reads all subsequent lines as `stdin` until it encounters that same delimiter word on a line by itself.

Syntax:

```
command << DELIMITER
Line 1 of input
Line 2 of input
... More lines ...
DELIMITER
```

The `DELIMITER` can be any word you choose (often `EOF` for End Of File, `END`, or something descriptive), just make sure it doesn't appear within the input text itself.

Let's feed multiple lines to `cat` using a here document:

```
$ cat << MY_DELIMITER
> This is the first line.
> This is the second line, provided directly.
> Isn't this neat?
> MY_DELIMITER
This is the first line.
This is the second line, provided directly.
Isn't this neat?
```

The > symbols on the continuation lines are prompts from the shell, indicating it's waiting for more input until it sees `MY_DELIMITER`.

Another example, counting the lines of input provided via a here document:

```
$ wc -l << EOF
> Mercury
> Venus
> Earth
> Mars
> EOF
      4
```

Here documents are especially useful inside shell scripts (which we'll start writing in Chapter 10) for providing configuration data or fixed text input to commands without needing separate files.

Here Strings (<<<)

A **Here String** is a simpler construct (available in Bash, Zsh, and some other modern shells, but not strictly POSIX standard) for providing a *single string* of text as standard input.

Syntax:

```
command <<< "Some string data"
```

This is often a more convenient alternative to using echo and a pipe (which we'll see next).

```
$ # Count words in a specific string
$ wc -w <<< "This is a test string."
      5

$ # Translate spaces to newlines in a string
$ tr ' ' '\n' <<< "Mercury Venus Earth Mars"
Mercury
Venus
Earth
Mars
```

While echo "string" | command achieves a similar result, <<< is slightly more efficient as it avoids creating an extra process just for the echo command.

Connecting Commands

Redirection connects commands to files. **Pipes**, represented by the vertical bar character |, connect the stdout of one command directly to the stdin of another command. This allows you to build powerful **pipelines**, chaining simple utilities together where the output of one becomes the input for the next, creating sophisticated data processing workflows.

Syntax:

```
command1 | command2 | command3 ...
```

Imagine an assembly line. command1 produces some output (its stdout). The pipe | acts as a conveyor belt, delivering that output directly to the input hopper (stdin) of command2. command2 processes that input and sends its output (stdout) down the next pipe | to command3, and so on. Only the final command in the pipeline typically writes its output to the terminal screen (unless it's also redirected).

Let's try some examples:

- **View long directory listing page by page:** ls -l produces many lines. We can pipe its output to less so we can view it one screenful at a time.

  ```
  $ ls -l /etc | less
  # Output of 'ls -l /etc' is displayed within the 'less' pager
  # Use spacebar/arrows to navigate, 'q' to quit less
  ```

  Here, ls doesn't write to the screen; its stdout goes directly into less's stdin.

- **Count the number of files in the current directory:**

  ```
  $ ls | wc -l # ls lists files (one per line usually), wc -l counts lines
      8
  ```

- **Find the number of unique planets in our file:** (Assuming celestial_bodies.txt might have duplicates)

  ```
  $ cat celestial_bodies.txt | sort | uniq | wc -l
      12 # Output depends on actual content and if duplicates existed
  ```

  - cat: Reads the file to stdout.

- sort: Reads stdin (from cat), sorts lines, writes sorted lines to stdout.
- uniq: Reads stdin (from sort), removes adjacent duplicate lines, writes unique lines to stdout.
- wc -l: Reads stdin (from uniq), counts lines, writes the count to stdout (the screen).

- **Find all running processes owned by user** jane:

```
$ ps aux | grep '^jane ' # ps aux lists all processes, grep filters
lines
jane      1234  0.0  0.1 ... some_process
jane      5678  0.2  0.5 ... another_process
```

- ps aux: Lists all running processes in detail to stdout.
- grep '^jane ': Reads stdin (from ps), finds lines starting (^) with "jane ", and prints those matching lines to stdout (the screen).

Important Pitfall: By default, pipes only connect stdout (1) to stdin (0). stderr (2) from the command on the left is *not* piped; it still goes to the screen (or wherever it was otherwise redirected).

```
$ find /etc -name hosts | grep avahi # Errors from find still go to screen
find: '/etc/cups/ssl': Permission denied
find: '/etc/polkit-1/rules.d': Permission denied
...
/etc/avahi/hosts # Grep finds this line from find's stdout
```

If you *want* to pipe both stdout and stderr together, you can use:

- |& **(Bash/Zsh shorthand):** Pipes both stdout and stderr.

```
$ find /etc -name hosts |& grep avahi # Pipes both stdout and stderr to
grep
/etc/avahi/hosts
```

(Note: Error messages containing "avahi" would also be matched here).

- 2>&1 | **(Traditional):** Redirect stderr to stdout *before* the pipe.

```
$ find /etc -name hosts 2>&1 | grep avahi # Redirect stderr, then pipe
/etc/avahi/hosts
```

Pipes are arguably one of the most powerful concepts in the Linux/UNIX philosophy: create simple tools that do one thing well, and then connect them together to solve complex problems.

Splitting Output

Sometimes, you want to save the output of a command to a file *and* see it on the screen simultaneously, or perhaps pass it further down a pipeline while also saving an intermediate copy. This is exactly what the `tee` command does.

Named after a T-shaped pipe fitting used in plumbing, `tee` reads from its standard input and writes that input to *both* standard output *and* one or more specified files.

Syntax:

```
command | tee output_file.txt | another_command
```

Let's list our playground contents, save the list to `file.log`, *and* view it with `less`:

```
$ ls -l
# (output appears in less pager)
$ ls -l | tee playground_list.log | less
# Now, after quitting less ('q')...
$ cat playground_list.log # The file also contains the ls output
total 20
drwx------ 2 jane jane 4096 Jul 23 16:05 Archive
drwxr-xr-x 2 jane science_proj 4096 Jul 23 15:35 LogsBackup
-rw-r--r-- 1 jane jane    0 Jul 23 16:00 mydata.txt
...
```

The output from `ls -l` went into `tee`. `tee` wrote a copy to `playground_list.log` *and* also wrote a copy to its own `stdout`. That `stdout` was then piped into `less` for viewing.

By default, `tee` overwrites the output file. To append instead, use the `-a` option:

```
$ date | tee -a system_events.log
Tue Jul 23 17:45:10 EDT 2024 # Output also goes to screen
$ whoami | tee -a system_events.log
jane # Output also goes to screen
$ cat system_events.log
Tue Jul 23 17:45:10 EDT 2024
jane
```

`tee` is invaluable for monitoring long-running processes while logging their output, or for saving intermediate results within complex pipelines without breaking the chain.

Chapter Summary

This chapter unlocked the power of controlling data flow on the command line. We started by understanding the three **standard streams**: `stdin` (0), `stdout` (1), and `stderr` (2). You learned how to redirect `stdout` to overwrite (>) or append (>>) to files, and how to capture `stderr` separately (2>, 2>>) or combine both streams (&>, > file 2>&1, &>>, >> file 2>&1). We then flipped the coin, redirecting `stdin` to read input *from* files using <. We explored convenient ways to provide input directly using **Here Documents** (<< DELIMITER) for multi-line input and **Here Strings** (<<< "string") for single strings. The highlight was learning how to connect commands using **pipes** (|), building powerful **pipelines** where the output of one command feeds the input of the next. Finally, we saw how `tee` lets us split a data stream, saving it to a file while simultaneously passing it along to the screen or the next command in a pipeline.

Mastering redirection and pipes transforms the command line from a simple command executor into a flexible data processing environment. You can now construct sophisticated workflows by combining simple utilities. With this ability to create potentially complex command sequences, our next step is to understand how Linux manages the programs, or **processes**, that these commands create. In Chapter 7, we'll dive into managing running processes – viewing them, controlling them, and running them in the background.

Managing Running Processes

In the last chapter, we unlocked the power of redirection and pipes, learning how to channel data between commands and files like a master plumber. You saw how combining simple commands (`ls | wc -l`) creates a more complex task. Each command you run, whether simple or part of a sophisticated pipeline, starts one or more **processes** on your system. A process is essentially a program in action. As you start running longer tasks, maybe a complex calculation or a file download, you'll realize you need ways to check on these running programs, manage them, and control whether they tie up your terminal or run quietly in the background. This chapter is your guide to becoming a process manager, teaching you how to view, control, and juggle the various tasks running on your Linux system.

What is a Process?

Think of a program like `ls` or `firefox` as a recipe stored in a cookbook (a file on your disk). When you actually decide to *run* that program, Linux creates a **process**. The process is like the chef actively following the recipe in the kitchen – it's the program in execution, using system resources like CPU time and memory to get the job done.

You can have multiple processes running the same program simultaneously. For instance, you could open several terminal windows; each window runs an instance of your shell program (like Bash), and each instance is a separate process. You could also run the same script multiple times concurrently; each run would be a distinct process.

To keep track of all these active "chefs," Linux assigns a unique identification number to each process, called the **Process ID** or **PID**. This PID is crucial for managing specific processes, like telling a particular chef to stop cooking. We'll use PIDs extensively in this chapter.

Viewing Processes

The fundamental command for viewing static information about the processes currently running is ps (short for **p**rocess **s**tatus). Running ps by itself usually isn't very informative, typically only showing processes associated with your current terminal session:

```
$ ps
  PID TTY          TIME CMD
 1234 pts/0    00:00:00 bash
 5678 pts/0    00:00:00 ps
```

This minimal output shows the PID, the controlling terminal (TTY), the accumulated CPU time used, and the command name (CMD). To get a useful, system-wide view, you need to use options. There are two main styles of options for ps, stemming from its historical roots in different UNIX variants: BSD style and System V style.

Common ps Options (BSD Style: aux)

One very popular and informative way to invoke ps uses BSD-style options (which don't require a leading hyphen). The combination ps aux is widely used:

- a: Show processes for **a**ll users.
- u: Display in a **u**ser-oriented format (shows the owner).
- x: Include processes not attached to any terminal (like system daemons or background tasks).

```
$ ps aux
USER        PID %CPU %MEM    VSZ    RSS TTY      STAT START   TIME COMMAND
root          1  0.0  0.1 169412  11628 ?        Ss   10:15   0:02 /sbin/init
splash
```

```
root            2  0.0  0.0       0     0 ?           S    10:15   0:00 [kthreadd]
root            3  0.0  0.0       0     0 ?           I<   10:15   0:00 [rcu_gp]
... *many system processes* ...
jane         1234  0.0  0.1   15880  7888 pts/0       Ss   11:20   0:00 /bin/bash
root         4501  0.1  0.2  350140 18140 ?           Sl   11:25   0:01
/usr/sbin/sshd -D
jane         5678  0.0  0.0   12345  3456 pts/0       R+   11:30   0:00 ps aux
```

Let's look at some key columns:

- **USER:** The user who owns the process.
- **PID:** The unique Process ID.
- **%CPU:** Approximate percentage of CPU time the process is currently using.
- **%MEM:** Approximate percentage of physical memory (RAM) the process is currently using.
- **VSZ:** Virtual Memory Size (total memory the process *might* use).
- **RSS:** Resident Set Size (how much physical memory it's *actually* occupying right now).
- **TTY:** Controlling terminal. ? means no controlling terminal.
- **STAT:** Process status code (e.g., S=Sleeping, R=Running, I=Idle, Z=Zombie, +=in foreground group).
- **START:** Time the process was started.
- **TIME:** Total accumulated CPU time used by the process.
- **COMMAND:** The command that launched the process (may be truncated).

This ps aux format gives a comprehensive snapshot of everything running on your system at that moment.

Common ps Options (System V Style: -ef)

Another common way to list all processes uses System V-style options (which require a leading hyphen). The combination ps -ef is also frequently used:

- -e: Show **e**very process.
- -f: Display a **f**ull-format listing (includes more details like PPID).

```
$ ps -ef
UID          PID    PPID  C STIME TTY          TIME CMD
root           1       0  0 10:15 ?        00:00:02 /sbin/init splash
root           2       0  0 10:15 ?        00:00:00 [kthreadd]
root           3       2  0 10:15 ?        00:00:00 [rcu_gp]
... *many system processes* ...
```

```
jane        1234    1200  0 11:20 pts/0    00:00:00 /bin/bash
root        4501       1  0 11:25 ?        00:00:01 /usr/sbin/sshd -D
jane        5680    1234  0 11:32 pts/0    00:00:00 ps -ef
```

Key columns in this format:

- **UID:** The username (often abbreviated).
- **PID:** The Process ID.
- **PPID:** The Parent Process ID. This is the PID of the process that *started* this process. This is very useful for understanding process relationships (e.g., your ps -ef command was likely started by your bash shell). Process 1 (init or systemd) is typically the ancestor of almost all other processes.
- **C:** CPU utilization (often simplified).
- **STIME:** Start time.
- **TTY:** Controlling terminal.
- **TIME:** Accumulated CPU time.
- **CMD:** The command.

Both ps aux and ps -ef give you a full view of the system's processes, just with slightly different information and formatting. Choose the one you find more readable or that provides the specific details (like PPID from -ef or %MEM from aux) you need. You'll often pipe the output of ps into grep to find specific processes, as we saw briefly in Chapter 6.

```
$ ps aux | grep firefox
jane       6001  5.2  8.5 2450120 350100 tty1    Sl+  11:40   0:15
/usr/lib/firefox/firefox
```

Interactive Process Viewing

While ps gives you a snapshot, sometimes you need a dynamic, real-time view of what your system is doing. This is where interactive process viewers like top and htop come in.

top

The top command provides a continuously updating display of system summary information and a list of the currently running processes, usually sorted by CPU usage by default.

```
$ top
```

The screen will clear and you'll see something like this:

```
top - 11:45:01 up 1:30,  2 users,  load average: 0.10, 0.18, 0.15
Tasks: 250 total,   1 running, 249 sleeping,   0 stopped,   0 zombie
%Cpu(s):  1.5 us,  0.8 sy,  0.0 ni, 97.5 id,  0.1 wa,  0.0 hi,  0.1 si,  0.0 st
MiB Mem :   7850.5 total,   4500.1 free,   2100.3 used,   1250.1 buff/cache
MiB Swap:   2048.0 total,   2048.0 free,      0.0 used.   5400.2 avail Mem

    PID USER      PR  NI    VIRT    RES    SHR S  %CPU  %MEM     TIME+ COMMAND
   6001 jane      20   0 2450120 350100  80500 S   5.1   8.5   0:25.10 firefox
   1234 jane      20   0   15880   7888   3400 S   0.3   0.1   0:01.50 bash
   4501 root      20   0  350140  18140   5100 S   0.1   0.2   0:02.10 sshd
      1 root      20   0  169412  11628   8000 S   0.0   0.1   0:02.05 init
      2 root      20   0       0      0      0 S   0.0   0.0   0:00.00 kthreadd
... *list continues and updates* ...
```

- **Top Section (Summary Area):** Shows system uptime, load averages, number of tasks, CPU states, memory usage (RAM), and swap usage.
- **Bottom Section (Process List):** Shows individual processes, similar to ps, but updating every few seconds (usually). Columns like PID, USER, %CPU, %MEM, and COMMAND are key.

Interacting with top:

- q: **Q**uit top.
- h: Show the help screen.
- k: **K**ill a process (prompts for PID and signal).
- r: **R**enice a process (change its priority, prompts for PID and nice value).
- Spacebar: Refresh the display immediately.
- **Sorting:**
  - Shift+P (P): Sort by %**CPU** usage (the default).
  - Shift+M (M): Sort by %**MEM** (memory) usage.
  - Shift+T (T): Sort by cumulative **TIME**.

top is a standard utility found on nearly every Linux system and is invaluable for quickly seeing what's consuming resources.

htop

htop is a popular, enhanced alternative to top. It provides a more visual, colorful, and often easier-to-use interface. You might need to install it first (sudo apt install htop on Debian/Ubuntu, sudo dnf install htop on Fedora/CentOS).

```
$ htop
```

htop typically displays:

- CPU meters (often per core) and memory/swap meters at the top.
- A scrollable list of processes, often color-coded.
- Function key shortcuts clearly listed at the bottom (F1 Help, F3 Search, F4 Filter, F5 Tree view, F9 Kill, F10 Quit).

Why htop is often preferred:

- **Scrolling:** You can scroll vertically and horizontally through the process list using arrow keys or PageUp/PageDown.
- **Easier Interaction:** Killing (F9), renicing (F7/F8), searching (F3), and filtering (F4) are more intuitive using function keys or menus.
- **Visuals:** Color coding and graphical meters make it easier to grasp system status quickly.
- **Tree View (F5):** Shows the parent-child relationships between processes clearly.

If htop is available on your system, it's generally a more pleasant tool for interactive process monitoring than top. Both achieve the same core goal, however.

Sending Signals to Processes

Viewing processes is one thing; controlling them is another. Often, you'll need to stop a misbehaving process or tell a service to reload its configuration. You do this by sending **signals** to the process.

A signal is a notification sent to a process to alert it of an event or instruct it to do something. Think of signals as predefined messages like "Please terminate," "Stop immediately," or "Reload your settings."

Common Signals

There are many signals defined, but these are the most frequently used:

- **SIGTERM (Signal number 15):** The **term**inate signal. This is the default signal sent by `kill` if you don't specify one. It's a polite request asking the process to shut down gracefully. Well-behaved programs will intercept this signal, save their work, close files, and exit cleanly.
- **SIGKILL (Signal number 9):** The **kill** signal. This is the hammer. SIGKILL cannot be caught or ignored by the process. The kernel immediately terminates the process, without giving it a chance to clean up. This should be used as a **last resort** when a process is completely unresponsive to SIGTERM, as it can lead to data loss or corruption if the process was writing files.
- **SIGHUP (Signal number 1):** The **hangup** signal. Historically used when a user disconnected via modem. Today, it's commonly used as a conventional signal to tell daemon processes (long-running background services) to **reload their configuration files** without fully restarting.
- **SIGINT (Signal number 2):** The **interrupt** signal. This is the signal sent when you press `Ctrl+C` in the terminal to stop a running foreground command.
- **SIGTSTP (Signal number 20):** The terminal **stop** signal. This is the signal sent when you press `Ctrl+Z` to suspend a foreground command (we'll cover this soon).

You can see a full list of signals available on your system with:

```
$ kill -l
 1) SIGHUP       2) SIGINT       3) SIGQUIT      4) SIGILL       5) SIGTRAP
 6) SIGABRT      7) SIGBUS       8) SIGFPE       9) SIGKILL     10) SIGUSR1
11) SIGSEGV     12) SIGUSR2     13) SIGPIPE     14) SIGALRM     15) SIGTERM
16) SIGSTKFLT   17) SIGCHLD     18) SIGCONT     19) SIGSTOP     20) SIGTSTP
... *list continues* ...
```

Using `kill`

The classic command for sending signals is `kill`. It requires the **PID** of the target process.

Syntax:

```
kill [options] [-SIGNAL] PID...
```

- -SIGNAL: Specifies the signal to send (e.g., -9, -KILL, -TERM, -15, -HUP). If omitted, SIGTERM (15) is sent by default.
- PID: The Process ID of the process(es) to signal.

Examples:

Let's say `firefox` has PID `6001` and is unresponsive.

1. **Try terminating gracefully first (SIGTERM):**

   ```
   $ kill 6001
   ```

   or explicitly:

   ```
   $ kill -TERM 6001
   $ kill -15 6001
   ```

   Wait a few seconds to see if the process exits. Check with `ps aux | grep firefox`.

2. **If it's still running, use the hammer (SIGKILL):**

   ```
   $ kill -KILL 6001
   ```

   or:

   ```
   $ kill -9 6001
   ```

   This should terminate it immediately.

3. **Tell a daemon with PID `7890` to reload its config (SIGHUP):**

   ```
   $ sudo kill -HUP 7890 # Often requires sudo for system daemons
   ```

Using `pkill` **and** `killall`

Finding the PID with `ps | grep` and then using `kill` can be tedious. `pkill` and `killall` let you send signals based on the process **name** or other attributes.

- `pkill`: Sends a signal to processes whose **name** (or other selected attribute) matches a pattern. By default, it sends SIGTERM.

```
$ # Terminate all processes named 'bad_program'
$ pkill bad_program

$ # Force kill (-9) all processes whose command line (-f) contains
'test_script.py'
$ pkill -9 -f test_script.py
```

Warning: pkill uses pattern matching. Be careful it doesn't match more processes than you intend! For example, pkill mail might kill evolution-mail-backend *and* thunderbird-mail.

- killall: Similar to pkill, but often matches the exact process name more strictly (behavior can vary slightly between systems). It also defaults to SIGTERM.

```
$ # Terminate all processes exactly named 'zombie_app'
$ killall zombie_app

$ # Ask all 'nginx' worker processes to reload config (-HUP)
$ sudo killall -HUP nginx
```

Warning: Like pkill, ensure the name is specific enough. killall bash could terminate *all* your shell sessions if run carelessly!

Both pkill and killall are convenient but require extra caution compared to using kill with a specific PID.

Running Commands in the Background

Normally, when you run a command in the terminal, it runs in the **foreground**. Your shell waits for the command to finish before displaying the prompt again, and you can't type new commands in the meantime. This is fine for quick commands like ls or pwd.

But what if you want to start a long-running task (like compressing a large file, running a complex script, or starting a graphical application) and immediately get your terminal prompt back so you can continue working? You can run the command in the **background** by appending an ampersand (&) to the end of the command line.

```
$ # This command would normally take 60 seconds
$ sleep 60 &
```

```
[1] 7123
$ # Prompt returns immediately! You can type other commands now.
```

When you run a command with &:

1. The shell starts the command.
2. It prints the **job number** (like [1]) and the **PID** (like 7123).
3. It immediately displays a new shell prompt, allowing you to enter more commands while sleep 60 continues running in the background.

Important: If a background command tries to read input from the terminal (stdin), it will usually be stopped. Also, background commands might still print their output (stdout and stderr) to your terminal, potentially interleaving with whatever you're typing. It's often a good idea to redirect the output of background tasks to files (as learned in Chapter 6):

```
$ ./my_long_script.sh > script.log 2>&1 &
[1] 7150
$ # Script runs in background, all output goes to script.log
```

Job Control

The shell provides features, collectively known as **job control**, to manage commands you've started, especially those running in the background or temporarily stopped.

Suspending Processes (Ctrl+Z)

What if you start a command in the foreground and then realize it's going to take a long time, but you forgot the &? You don't have to kill it! Pressing Ctrl+Z sends the SIGTSTP signal to the currently running *foreground* process, **suspending** it. The process is paused, not terminated, and you get your shell prompt back.

```
$ sleep 100 # Started in foreground, ties up terminal
^Z # Pressed Ctrl+Z
[1]+  Stopped                 sleep 100
$ # Prompt returns, 'sleep 100' is paused.
```

The shell prints the job number ([1]), its status (Stopped), and the command.

Listing Jobs

To see the commands currently managed by your shell (those running in the background or suspended), use the jobs command:

```
$ # Assuming we have the suspended sleep and maybe another background task
$ ./another_script.sh &
[2] 7201
$ jobs
[1]+  Stopped                 sleep 100
[2]-  Running                 ./another_script.sh &
```

The output shows:

- Job number ([1], [2]).
- A + indicates the "current" job (the one fg or bg would affect by default).
- A - indicates the "previous" job.
- The status (Stopped, Running).
- The command.

Resuming in Background

To take a *suspended* job (like our sleep 100) and let it continue running *in the background*, use the bg (background) command, followed by the job identifier (usually % and the job number).

```
$ jobs
[1]+  Stopped                 sleep 100
[2]-  Running                 ./another_script.sh &
$ bg %1
[1]+ sleep 100 &
$ jobs
[1]+  Running                 sleep 100 &
[2]-  Running                 ./another_script.sh &
```

Now sleep 100 is running again, but in the background, freeing up your terminal. If you omit the job ID, bg usually operates on the job marked with +.

Bringing to Foreground

To bring a job that is running in the background *or* is suspended back to the **foreground**, use the fg (foreground) command, again followed by the job identifier.

```
$ jobs
[1]+  Running                 sleep 100 &
[2]-  Running                 ./another_script.sh &
$ fg %1 # Bring sleep 100 back to the foreground
sleep 100
# Terminal is now waiting for sleep 100 to finish...
# (or you could press Ctrl+Z again)
```

Now sleep 100 is running in the foreground again, and your shell prompt won't return until it finishes or you suspend/kill it. If you omit the job ID, fg usually operates on the job marked with +.

Mastering job control (&, Ctrl+Z, jobs, fg, bg) gives you tremendous flexibility in managing how commands run in your interactive shell sessions.

Chapter Summary

In this chapter, you learned how to interact with the programs running on your system. We defined a **process** as a running instance of a program, each identified by a unique **PID**. You learned how to view static snapshots of processes using ps (with common options aux or -ef) and how to monitor them dynamically in real-time using top and the enhanced htop. We explored the concept of **signals** as messages sent to processes and learned how to use kill, pkill, and killall to send signals like SIGTERM (terminate gracefully), SIGKILL (terminate forcefully), and SIGHUP (reload configuration). Finally, you mastered **job control**, learning how to run commands in the **background** (&), **suspend** foreground commands (Ctrl+Z), list current jobs (jobs), resume jobs in the background (bg), and bring them back to the **foreground** (fg).

You now have the tools not just to run commands, but to observe and manage them effectively while they execute. This control, combined with the redirection techniques from Chapter 6, sets the stage for tailoring your command-line environment exactly to your liking. In the next chapter, we'll explore how to customize your shell environment using variables, aliases, and startup files to make your command-line experience even more powerful and efficient.

8

Customizing Your Shell Environment

So far, you've navigated the Linux landscape, managed files, viewed their contents, understood permissions, wrestled with processes, and even bent data streams to your will using redirection and pipes. You're getting proficient with individual commands. But what if you could make the shell itself work *smarter* for you? What if you could teach it shortcuts, make it remember things, or even change the way it greets you? That's exactly what this chapter is about. We're moving beyond just *using* the shell to actively *customizing* it. We'll explore variables that store information, aliases that create command shortcuts, startup files that run commands automatically, ways to recall previous commands efficiently, and how to personalize that command prompt you see constantly. Get ready to tailor your command-line environment to fit *your* work-flow.

Shell Variables vs. Environment Variables

The shell needs a way to keep track of information – things like your username, your home directory, the directories where executable programs are located, or even temporary values you define yourself. It does this using **variables**. Think of a variable as a named container or label that holds a piece of data (usually text).

There are two main types of variables you'll interact with in the shell:

1. **Shell Variables:** These variables exist *only* within the specific instance of the shell where they were created. They are local to that shell session. If you start another shell session (e.g., open a new terminal window), it won't know about the shell variables created in the first one. Imagine settings you adjust on a specific machine in a factory – they only affect *that* machine.
2. **Environment Variables:** These variables are not only available to the current shell but are also **passed down** to any *child processes* started by that shell. Child processes are commands or scripts you run from the shell. This makes environment variables suitable for storing system-wide settings or information that other programs might need to access. Think of these as factory-wide announcements or settings that affect all machines started within the factory.

The distinction is crucial: shell variables are local; environment variables are inherited by commands you run.

Viewing Variables

How do you see these variables? There are several commands:

set

The set command, when run without arguments, displays a comprehensive list of **all** shell variables (including environment variables, shell-specific variables, and even shell functions). The output can be quite long!

```
$ set
BASH=/bin/bash
BASHOPTS=checkwinsize:cmdhist:expand_aliases:extglob:extquote:force_fignore:hist
append:interactive_comments:login_shell:progcomp:promptvars:sourcepath
BASH_ALIASES=()
BASH_ARGC=()
...
# Lots of Bash-specific variables (starting with BASH_)
...
# Environment variables like HOME, PATH, USER
HOME=/home/jane
HOSTNAME=my-linux-box
...
# Shell variables you might have defined
my_variable='hello there'
...
```

```
# Shell functions might also be listed
ls ()
{
    command ls --color=auto "$@"
}
... *output truncated* ...
```

You'll see environment variables (usually in uppercase like HOME, PATH), many internal shell variables (often uppercase or starting with BASH_), and any variables or functions you've defined yourself.

env **or** printenv

To see *only* the **environment variables** – those that are passed down to child processes – use the env or printenv commands. They typically produce identical, cleaner output compared to set.

```
$ env
SHELL=/bin/bash
SESSION_MANAGER=local/my-linux-box:@/tmp/.ICE-unix/1234,unix/my-linux-box:/
tmp/.ICE-unix/1234
QT_ACCESSIBILITY=1
COLORTERM=truecolor
XDG_CONFIG_DIRS=/etc/xdg/xdg-ubuntu:/etc/xdg
SSH_AGENT_PID=5678
XDG_MENU_PREFIX=gnome-
USER=jane
PWD=/home/jane/playground
HOME=/home/jane
SSH_AUTH_SOCK=/run/user/1001/keyring/ssh
EMAIL=jane@example.com # Example environment variable
XDG_SESSION_TYPE=x11
XDG_DATA_DIRS=/usr/share/ubuntu:/usr/local/share/:/usr/share/:/var/lib/snapd/
desktop
PATH=/home/jane/bin:/usr/local/sbin:/usr/local/bin:/usr/sbin:/usr/bin:/sbin:/bin
DBUS_SESSION_BUS_ADDRESS=unix:path=/run/user/1001/bus
TERM=xterm-256color
... *output truncated* ...
```

This list is shorter than set's output because it only includes variables that child processes will inherit. printenv often gives the exact same output. You can also give printenv a specific variable name to see just its value:

```
$ printenv HOME
/home/jane
$ printenv PATH
/home/jane/bin:/usr/local/sbin:/usr/local/bin:/usr/sbin:/usr/bin:/sbin:/bin
```

echo

The most common way to view the value of a *specific* variable (shell or environment) is using the echo command followed by a dollar sign ($) and the variable name. The $ tells the shell to substitute the variable's name with its stored value *before* running the echo command.

```
$ echo $USER
jane
$ echo $HOME
/home/jane
$ echo $HOSTNAME
my-linux-box
$ echo $SHELL
/bin/bash
```

If you try to echo a variable that doesn't exist, it usually just prints an empty line:

```
$ echo $non_existent_variable

$ # (empty line)
```

Creating and Setting Variables

You can easily create your own variables in the shell. Variable names typically consist of letters, numbers, and underscores (_), and conventionally start with a letter. They are **case-sensitive** (myvar is different from MyVar).

To assign a value, use the equals sign (=). **Crucially, there must be no spaces around the equals sign.**

```
$ # Correct: no spaces
$ my_location="New York"
$ count=10

$ # Incorrect: spaces around =
```

```
$ my_city = "London"
bash: my_city: command not found...

$ # Now let's check our variables
$ echo $my_location
New York
$ echo $count
10
```

Notice the quotes around "New York". Quotes are important when the value contains spaces or special characters. We'll dive deeper into quoting in Chapter 11 when we discuss scripting, but for simple assignments:

- Use double quotes ("...") if the value has spaces. Variables inside double quotes *are* expanded (e.g., echo "My home is $HOME" works).
- Use single quotes ('...') if the value has spaces and you want *no* variable expansion or special character interpretation (e.g., echo 'My home is $HOME' prints the literal $HOME).
- No quotes are needed for simple values without spaces or special characters.

By default, variables created this way are **shell variables**, local to the current shell.

```
$ my_shell_var="Local only"
$ echo $my_shell_var
Local only
$ bash # Start a new, nested bash shell
$ echo $my_shell_var # Try to access it in the child shell

$ # (empty line - the child shell doesn't know about it)
$ exit # Exit the nested shell
$ echo $my_shell_var # Back in the original shell
Local only
```

Making Variables Global

How do you turn a local shell variable into an environment variable that child processes can inherit? You use the export command.

You can either define and export in one step:

```
$ export API_KEY="a1b2c3d4e5f6"
$ export EDITOR="nano"
```

Or define it first, then export it later:

```
$ MY_SETTING="enabled"
$ export MY_SETTING
```

Now, let's re-run our test with the nested shell:

```
$ export GLOBAL_VAR="Visible everywhere"
$ echo $GLOBAL_VAR
Visible everywhere
$ bash # Start a new child shell
$ echo $GLOBAL_VAR # Check if it's visible here
Visible everywhere # Yes! It was inherited.
$ exit # Exit child shell
```

Because we used `export`, `GLOBAL_VAR` became an environment variable and was passed down to the child `bash` process.

You can see exported variables using `env` or `printenv`:

```
$ env | grep GLOBAL_VAR
GLOBAL_VAR=Visible everywhere
```

Why export variables? Many programs look for specific environment variables to configure their behavior. For instance:

- `EDITOR`: Specifies the default text editor programs might call (like `nano` or `vim`).
- `PAGER`: Specifies the default pager program (like `less`).
- `HTTP_PROXY`: Configures proxy settings for network connections.
- Application-specific variables (e.g., `JAVA_HOME` for Java applications).

Setting and exporting these allows you to customize how other commands operate within your session.

The Command Search Path

Have you ever wondered how, when you type `ls` or `pwd` or `nano`, the shell knows *where* to find the actual executable program file for that command? It doesn't magically know about every program on your system. Instead, it searches through a specific list of directories defined by the `PATH` **environment variable**.

The `PATH` variable contains a colon-separated (:) list of directories. When you type a command name without specifying a full path (like `/bin/ls`), the shell looks for an executable file with that name in each directory listed in `PATH`, in order, until it finds one.

```
$ echo $PATH
/home/jane/bin:/usr/local/sbin:/usr/local/bin:/usr/sbin:/usr/bin:/sbin:/bin:/
usr/games:/usr/local/games:/snap/bin
```

In this example, the shell would first look in `/home/jane/bin`, then `/usr/local/sbin`, then `/usr/local/bin`, and so on. The first place it finds an executable named `ls` (likely `/bin/ls` or `/usr/bin/ls`), it stops searching and runs that program. If it searches all directories in `PATH` and doesn't find the command, you get the familiar "command not found" error.

Adding to the `PATH`

Sometimes you might install software manually or write your own scripts and place them in a directory not listed in the default `PATH` (like `~/scripts`). To run these scripts by just typing their name (e.g., `my_backup_script`) instead of the full path (`~/scripts/my_backup_script`), you need to add their directory to your `PATH`.

You can do this temporarily for the current session:

```
$ # Assuming your scripts are in /home/jane/scripts
$ export PATH="$PATH:/home/jane/scripts"

$ # Now verify the change
$ echo $PATH
/home/jane/bin:/usr/local/sbin: ... :/snap/bin:/home/jane/scripts # Added at the
end

$ # Now you can run scripts in that directory by name (if they are executable)
$ my_backup_script
```

Explanation:

- `export PATH=...`: We need `export` because we want child processes (the commands we run) to inherit the updated `PATH`.
- `"$PATH:/home/jane/scripts"`: This is crucial. We take the *existing* value of `PATH` (`$PATH`), add a colon (:), and then append our new directory (`/home/jane/scripts`). The double quotes are important to handle potential spaces or

special characters in existing path elements. **Never just do** `export PATH="/home/jane/scripts"` as that would *replace* the entire existing path, making most standard commands unusable! You almost always want to *append* or *prepend* to the existing `$PATH`.

To make this change permanent, you need to add the `export PATH=...` line to one of your shell startup files, which we'll discuss next.

Shell Startup Files

When you start a shell session (by logging in or opening a terminal window), Bash automatically executes commands from specific configuration files, often called startup or initialization files. This is where you put customizations like setting environment variables (`export PATH=...`), defining aliases, or setting shell options that you want to apply every time you start a shell.

The exact files used depend on whether the shell is started as a **login shell** or an **interactive non-login shell**. This distinction often causes confusion, so let's clarify:

- **Login Shell:** A shell session you start by actually logging into the system. Examples:
    - Logging in on a text-based console (tty).
    - Logging in remotely via SSH (`ssh user@host`).
    - Using `su -l` or `su -` to switch user.
    - Sometimes, the *first* terminal window opened after graphical login might act as a login shell (depends on the terminal emulator and system configuration).
- **Interactive Non-Login Shell:** A shell session started *after* you've already logged in, without re-authenticating. Examples:
    - Opening a new terminal window in a graphical desktop environment (most common case).
    - Running `bash` explicitly from an existing shell.
    - Running a script interactively (though script environments differ).

Why the difference? Login shells are meant for one-time setup upon login (like setting environment variables that should persist for the entire session), while non-login shells might need slightly different or less setup for each interactive session (like defining aliases specific to terminal use).

Here are the main startup files Bash typically looks for:

1. **Login Shells:**

- Reads /etc/profile first (system-wide settings, applied to all users).
- Then looks for the *first one it finds* of these in your home directory and reads *only that one*:
    - ~/.bash_profile (Most common personal login file)
    - ~/.bash_login
    - ~/.profile (Generic, also used by other shells like sh, ksh. Often used if the others don't exist).

2. **Interactive Non-Login Shells:**

- Reads /etc/bash.bashrc (system-wide settings for interactive shells, if it exists).
- Reads ~/.bashrc in your home directory (Most common personal interactive, non-login file).

The Common Pattern: Because users typically want most of their settings (like aliases and PATH adjustments) applied to *both* login and interactive non-login shells, a very common practice is to put most customizations into ~/.bashrc and then have ~/.bash_profile (or ~/.profile) *source* (execute) ~/.bashrc.

You might see lines like this inside your ~/.bash_profile or ~/.profile:

```
# if running bash
if [ -n "$BASH_VERSION" ]; then
    # include .bashrc if it exists
    if [ -f "$HOME/.bashrc" ]; then
        . "$HOME/.bashrc" # The dot '.' is the source command
    fi
fi
```

This ensures that when you log in (which reads .bash_profile), it also executes the commands in .bashrc. Subsequent terminal windows (non-login) will just read .bashrc directly.

Where to Put Your Customizations:

- **For environment variables** (export VAR=..., export PATH=...): Traditionally put in ~/.bash_profile (or ~/.profile). This ensures they are set once upon login and inherited by all subsequent processes (including graphical applications started after login). If your .bash_profile sources .bashrc, putting them in .bashrc inside a check (if ! [["$PATH" =~ ...]]) might also work, but .bash_profile is often considered cleaner for things set only once per login.

- **For aliases, shell options (`set -o`), and prompt settings (`PS1`):** Put these in `~/.bashrc`. These are generally most useful in interactive terminal sessions.

Applying Changes: After editing a startup file (e.g., `nano ~/.bashrc`), the changes won't take effect until you start a *new* shell session. To apply them to your *current* session, you can use the `source` command (or its shortcut, the dot `.`) to execute the file directly:

```
$ source ~/.bashrc
```

or

```
$ . ~/.bashrc
```

Creating Shortcuts

Do you find yourself typing the same long command or combination of options frequently? For example, maybe you always use `ls -alh` instead of just `ls`. You can create shortcuts for commands using **aliases**. An alias is simply a user-defined nickname for a command string.

Defining Aliases

Use the `alias` command to define a new alias.

Syntax:

```
alias name='command_string'
```

Again, no spaces around the `=`. The `command_string` should be enclosed in single quotes (`'`) to prevent immediate expansion of special characters or variables, unless you specifically need expansion *at the time the alias is defined*.

Examples:

```
$ # Create a shortcut for detailed, human-readable, all-files listing
$ alias ll='ls -alh'

$ # Create a shortcut for updating system packages (example for Debian/Ubuntu)
$ alias update='sudo apt update && sudo apt upgrade -y'
```

```
$ # Create a shortcut to go up one directory
$ alias ..='cd ..'

$ # Create a shortcut to clear the screen
$ alias cls='clear'
```

Now you can just type the alias name instead of the full command:

```
$ ll # Runs ls -alh
total 32K
drwxr-xr-x 7 jane jane 4.0K Jul 23 17:30 .
drwxr-xr-x 3 root root 4.0K Jul 20 10:00 ..
drwx------ 2 jane jane 4.0K Jul 23 16:05 Archive
...

$ update # Runs sudo apt update && sudo apt upgrade -y
[sudo] password for jane:
... package update output ...

$ .. # Runs cd ..
$ pwd
/home/jane
```

To see all currently defined aliases, run alias without arguments:

```
$ alias
alias ..='cd ..'
alias cls='clear'
alias ll='ls -alh'
alias update='sudo apt update && sudo apt upgrade -y'
# ... plus any default aliases your distribution might provide
```

Removing Aliases

To remove an alias you no longer need, use the unalias command:

```
$ unalias cls
$ alias | grep cls # Verify it's gone
```

Persistence

Aliases defined directly in the shell only last for the current session. To make them permanent, add the `alias` definition lines to your `~/.bashrc` file. This way, they'll be loaded every time you start an interactive shell.

Potential Pitfall: Be careful not to create aliases with the same name as existing essential commands unless you *really* mean to override them (e.g., `alias rm='rm -i'` is a common safety alias, but `alias cd='echo Cannot change directory'` would be problematic!). If you need to run the original command instead of its alias, you can bypass the alias by:

- Prefixing the command with a backslash: `\ls`
- Using the full path: `/bin/ls`
- Using the `command` built-in: `command ls`

Recalling Previous Commands

The shell remembers the commands you type, which is incredibly useful for avoiding retyping long or complex commands. This feature is called **history**.

Viewing History

The `history` command displays a numbered list of the commands you've recently executed:

```
$ history
    1  cd playground/
    2  ls
    3  mkdir TestDir
    4  touch TestDir/file{1..3}.txt
    5  ls -l TestDir/
    6  cat planets.txt
    7  alias ll='ls -alh'
    8  ll
    9  history
```

The number of commands stored is controlled by shell variables like `HISTSIZE` (number kept in memory during the session) and `HISTFILESIZE` (number saved to the history file, usually `~/.bash_history`, when you exit).

Re-executing Commands

The ! character allows you to re-execute commands from your history:

- !!: Execute the **last** command again.
- !n: Execute command number n from the history list (e.g., !5 would run ls -l TestDir/ in the example above).
- !-n: Execute the command n lines back from the current one (e.g., !-1 is the same as !!, !-2 executes the second-to-last command).
- !string: Execute the most recent command starting with string (e.g., !cat would run cat planets.txt).
- !?string?: Execute the most recent command containing string.

Warning: Using ! can sometimes be risky if you're not sure *exactly* which command it will match, especially with !string. Always be careful when re-executing commands that modify or delete things!

Searching History

A much safer and often more efficient way to find and re-execute previous commands is using **reverse-i-search** by pressing Ctrl+R.

1. Press Ctrl+R. Your prompt changes to something like (reverse-i-search)`.
2. Start typing characters from the command you want to find. The shell will instantly show the most recent match containing the characters you've typed so far.
3. Keep typing to refine the search, or press Ctrl+R again to cycle backward through older matches containing the same characters.
4. Once you see the command you want:
   - Press Enter to execute it immediately.
   - Press Right Arrow or Left Arrow (or Ctrl+E, Ctrl+A) to place the command on the current prompt line for editing before execution.
   - Press Ctrl+G or Ctrl+C to cancel the search.

Ctrl+R is arguably the single most useful history feature for interactive use. Practice using it!

Navigating History

You can also usually use the **Up Arrow** and **Down Arrow** keys to scroll backward and forward through your command history one command at a time.

Making Your Prompt Your Own

The text string that the shell displays to indicate it's ready for a command is called the **prompt**. Its appearance is controlled by a special shell variable called PS1. By customizing PS1, you can make your prompt more informative or visually appealing.

```
$ echo $PS1
\[\e]0;\u@\h: \w\a\]${debian_chroot:+($debian_chroot)}\[\033[01;32m\]\u@\h\[\
033[00m\]:\[\033[01;34m\]\w\[\033[00m\]\$
```

The default PS1 often looks complicated because it includes non-printing characters (like \[...\]) for terminal control sequences (like setting colors or the window title). However, the core components use special backslash-escaped characters:

- \u: Your **u**sername.
- \h: The **h**ostname (up to the first dot).
- \H: The full **H**ostname.
- \w: The current **w**orking directory (full path, ~ abbreviation used for home).
- \W: The basename of the current **W**orking directory (just the last part).
- \$: Displays a # if you are the root user, otherwise a $.
- \d: The **d**ate in "Weekday Month Date" format.
- \t: The **t**ime in HH:MM:SS format (24-hour).
- \n: A **n**ewline character.
- \@: Current time, 12-hour AM/PM format.
- \s: The name of the **s**hell.

Let's create a simpler prompt: username@hostname:current_directory $

```
$ export PS1='\u@\h:\w\$ ' # Remember the trailing space!

jane@my-linux-box:~/playground$ cd /etc
jane@my-linux-box:/etc$ cd ~
jane@my-linux-box:~$
```

To add a newline before the prompt for better separation:

```
$ export PS1='\n\u@\h:\w\n\$ '

jane@my-linux-box:~/playground

$ cd /var/log
```

```
jane@my-linux-box:/var/log

$
```

Adding colors requires embedding ANSI escape codes within \[and \] (to tell Bash they don't take up space on the line). This can get complex quickly. Many online "Bash PS1 generators" can help you create colorful prompts.

Example of a simple green username@hostname:

```
# Green: \[\033[0;32m\] Reset: \[\033[0m\]
$ export PS1='\[\033[0;32m\]\u@\h\[\033[0m\]:\w\$ '

jane@my-linux-box:~/playground$ # Prompt is now green
```

Like aliases and other variables, set your desired PS1 in your ~/.bashrc file to make it permanent for interactive sessions. Experiment to find a prompt that gives you the information you find most useful!

Chapter Summary

In this chapter, you learned how to mold your shell environment to your preferences. We distinguished between local **shell variables** and inherited **environment variables**, and saw how to view them (set, env, echo $VAR) and create them, using export to make them available to child processes. You now understand the critical role of the $PATH variable in command discovery and how to modify it. We navigated the often-confusing world of shell **startup files** (/etc/profile, ~/.bash_profile, ~/.profile, /etc/bash.bashrc, ~/.bashrc), clarifying the difference between login and non-login shells and the common practice of sourcing .bashrc from .bash_profile. You learned to create command shortcuts with **aliases** (alias, unalias) and efficiently reuse previous commands using **history** (history, !, and especially Ctrl+R). Finally, you discovered how to personalize your command **prompt** by customizing the PS1 variable.

Your shell is no longer just a tool; it's becoming *your* tool, configured the way you like it. With this customized environment and your knowledge of commands, pipes, and processes, you're well-prepared to tackle more complex tasks. Next, we'll focus on a set of indispensable command-line utilities specifically designed for processing and manipulating text – the bread and butter of many command-line operations. Chapter 9 introduces powerful tools like `grep`, `sed`, and `awk`.

9

Essential Text Processing Tools

Having learned how to navigate, manage files, handle permissions, control processes, and customize your environment, you're becoming quite skilled at interacting with the Linux system. A huge part of working effectively on the command line involves dealing with text – configuration files are text, log files are text, the output of many commands is text, and data often comes in text formats. Being able to search, filter, modify, and transform this text directly from the command line is a superpower. This chapter introduces you to a core set of indispensable Linux utilities designed precisely for this purpose. We'll meet `grep` for finding patterns, `sed` for editing streams, `awk` for powerful field manipulation, and others like `sort`, `wc`, `uniq`, `tr`, `diff`, `cut`, and `paste`. These tools often form the heart of command pipelines (remember Chapter 6?), allowing you to slice, dice, and reshape text data with remarkable efficiency.

Finding Text Patterns

Perhaps the most famous text-processing tool is `grep` (**g**lobal **r**egular **e**xpression **p**rint). Its job is simple but essential: search for lines containing a specified pattern within files or standard input, and print the matching lines. Need to find every occurrence of an error message in a log file? Need to see which configuration file mentions a specific setting? `grep` is your go-to tool.

The basic syntax is:

```
grep [options] PATTERN [file...]
```

- PATTERN: The text or pattern you're searching for.
- file...: One or more files to search within. If no files are specified, grep reads from standard input (making it perfect for pipelines).

Let's use our celestial_bodies.txt file from Chapter 4:

```
$ cd ~/playground
$ cat celestial_bodies.txt
Mercury
Venus
Earth
Mars
Jupiter
Saturn
Uranus
Neptune
Pluto (Dwarf Planet)
Our Moon
Phobos
Deimos

$ # Find lines containing "Planet"
$ grep Planet celestial_bodies.txt
Pluto (Dwarf Planet)
```

grep found the line containing "Planet" and printed it.

Key grep Options:

- -i (Ignore Case): Performs a case-insensitive search.

  ```
  $ grep mars celestial_bodies.txt # No output (case-sensitive)
  $ grep -i mars celestial_bodies.txt
  Mars
  ```

- -v (Invert Match): Prints lines that *do not* contain the pattern.

  ```
  $ # Show lines NOT containing 'Moon' or 'Planet'
  $ grep -v -e Moon -e Planet celestial_bodies.txt # Use -e for multiple
  patterns
  ```

```
Mercury
Venus
Earth
Mars
Jupiter
Saturn
Uranus
Neptune
Phobos
Deimos
```

(Note: -e *allows specifying multiple patterns. Alternatively,* grep -v 'Moon\|
Planet' celestial_bodies.txt *might work with basic regular expressions,
depending on the* grep *version).*

- -n (Line Number): Shows the line number in the file before each matching
  line.

  ```
  $ grep -n Saturn celestial_bodies.txt
  6:Saturn
  ```

- -r or -R (Recursive): Searches for the pattern in all files within the specified
  directory and its subdirectories.

  ```
  $ # Search recursively in the current directory (.) for 'jane'
  $ grep -r jane .
  ./activity.log:jane
  ./all_output.log:find: '/etc/polkit-1/rules.d': Permission denied #
  Example output
  ./all_output.log:find: '/etc/audit': Permission denied
  ./playground_contents.txt:drwxr-xr-x 2 jane jane 4096 Jul 23 16:05 Notes
  ...
  ```

- -c (Count): Instead of printing matching lines, just prints a count of how many
  lines matched.

  ```
  $ grep -c Moon celestial_bodies.txt
  1
  ```

- -w (Word Regexp): Only matches whole words. For example, grep -w 'on'
  would match the line "Turn the heating on" but not "Monday".

```
$ grep on celestial_bodies.txt
Venus
Our Moon
$ grep -w on celestial_bodies.txt # Doesn't match 'Venus' or 'Moon'
```

- **-E (Extended Regex)**: Interprets the PATTERN as an extended regular expression. Regular expressions are incredibly powerful pattern-matching languages involving special metacharacters (like *, +, ?, [], (), |). We'll dedicate **Chapter 16** to exploring them thoroughly. For now, just know that -E enables more complex patterns.

Using grep in Pipelines:

grep truly shines when filtering the output of other commands.

```
$ # Find processes related to 'bash'
$ ps aux | grep bash
jane          1234  0.0  0.1  15880  7888 pts/0     Ss+   11:20     0:01 /bin/bash
jane          8001  0.0  0.0  12000  3000 pts/1     S+    18:05     0:00 grep bash

$ # List only text files in the current directory
$ ls -l | grep '^-.*\.txt$' # Use basic regex: start '-', any chars, '.txt', end
'$'
-rw-r--r-- 1 jane jane    0 Jul 23 16:00 mydata.txt
-rw-r--r-- 1 jane jane  114 Jul 23 14:05 planets.txt
-rw-r--r-- 1 jane jane  349 Jul 23 16:45 playground_contents.txt
```

grep is your fundamental tool for finding needles of text within haystacks of data.

Editing Streams of Text

While grep finds lines, sed (stream **ed**itor) modifies them. It reads text from standard input or files, performs specified editing operations on each line, and sends the modified result to standard output. It doesn't (by default) change the original file; it just transforms the stream passing through it.

The most common use of sed by far is for **substitution** using the s command.

Substitution Syntax:

```
sed [options] 's/FIND_PATTERN/REPLACEMENT_STRING/FLAGS' [file...]
```

- s: Indicates the substitute command.
- /: Acts as a delimiter (you can often use other characters like # or | if your pattern contains slashes).
- FIND_PATTERN: The text or regular expression to find.
- REPLACEMENT_STRING: The text to replace the found pattern with.
- FLAGS (Optional): Modify the substitution behavior. Common flags:
    - g (Global): Replace *all* occurrences of the pattern on the line, not just the first one.
    - i (Ignore Case): Perform case-insensitive matching (GNU sed extension).
    - N (Number): Replace only the Nth occurrence on the line.

Examples:

```
$ # Replace 'Planet' with 'World' in our file (only first occurrence per line)
$ sed 's/Planet/World/' celestial_bodies.txt
Mercury
Venus
Earth
Mars
Jupiter
Saturn
Uranus
Neptune
Pluto (Dwarf World) # Changed!
Our Moon
Phobos
Deimos

$ # Let's try replacing 'u' with 'X' globally on each line
$ sed 's/u/X/g' celestial_bodies.txt
MercXry
VenXs
Earth
Mars
JXpiter
SatXrn
UranXs
NeptXne
PlXto (Dwarf Planet)
OXr Moon
Phobos
Deimos

$ # Change the first colon in /etc/passwd to a TAB (using | as delimiter)
```

```
$ head -n 1 /etc/passwd | sed 's|:|    |' # Using TAB character directly
root     x:0:0:root:/root:/bin/bash
```

In-Place Editing (-i):

Sometimes you *do* want to modify the original file. sed provides the -i option for this. **Use with extreme caution!** It's highly recommended to create a backup first, or use -i.bak which creates a backup of the original file with a .bak extension before modifying it.

```
$ cp celestial_bodies.txt planets_backup.txt # Manual backup
$ sed -i 's/Mars/Red Planet/' celestial_bodies.txt # Modify in-place
$ cat celestial_bodies.txt
Mercury
Venus
Earth
Red Planet # Changed in the original file!
Jupiter
...

$ # Using built-in backup
$ sed -i.bak 's/Saturn/Ringed Planet/' celestial_bodies.txt
$ cat celestial_bodies.txt # Shows 'Ringed Planet'
...
Saturn # Original content replaced
...
$ cat celestial_bodies.txt.bak # Backup file exists
...
Saturn # Original line preserved
...
```

While sed can do much more (like deleting lines with d, printing specific lines with p and -n), substitution (s) is its most frequent application and a powerful tool for quick text replacements in files or pipelines.

A Powerful Text Processor

awk is another giant in the world of Linux text processing. Named after its creators (Aho, Weinberger, and Kernighan), awk is much more than just a simple filter; it's a complete pattern-scanning and processing language. While grep selects lines and sed edits lines, awk excels at working with **fields** (columns) within lines. If your text has some structure, like columns separated by spaces, tabs, or other delimiters, awk is often the best tool for the job.

Basic Concept: awk reads its input (from files or stdin) one line at a time. For each line, it automatically splits the line into fields based on a **field separator** (whitespace by default). It then checks the line against optional patterns you provide. If a line matches a pattern, awk executes the corresponding { action } block.

Basic Syntax:

```
awk [options] 'pattern { action }' [file...]
```

- options: Common options include -F DELIMITER to specify the field separator.
- pattern: An expression that determines if the action should run for the current line (e.g., a comparison, a regular expression match). If omitted, the action runs for every line.
- { action }: One or more statements telling awk what to do (e.g., print fields, perform calculations, modify variables).

Built-in Variables (Inside the { action }):

- $0: Represents the entire current input line.
- $1, $2, $3, ...: Represent the first, second, third, etc., field on the current line.
- NF: **N**umber of **F**ields on the current line.
- NR: **N**umber of the **R**ecord (the current line number) processed so far.
- FS: **F**ield **S**eparator character (can be set with -F).
- OFS: **O**utput **F**ield **S**eparator (space by default, controls how print separates items).

Examples:

Let's create a simple file data.txt:

```
Item1   100   active
Item2   50    inactive
Item3   250   active
Item4   15    active
```

- **Print the first and third columns:**

```
$ awk '{ print $1, $3 }' data.txt
```

```
Item1 active
Item2 inactive
Item3 active
Item4 active
```

- **Print lines where the second column (value) is greater than 60:**

```
$ awk '$2 > 60 { print $0 }' data.txt # $2 > 60 is the pattern
Item1   100   active
Item3   250   active
```

- **Calculate the sum of the second column:**

```
$ awk '{ sum += $2 } END { print "Total:", sum }' data.txt
Total: 415
```

  - `{ sum += $2 }`: This action runs for every line, adding the value of the second field to the sum variable.
  - `END { ... }`: This is a special pattern that runs *after* all input lines have been processed.
- **Print usernames and shells from** /etc/passwd **(using ':' as delimiter):**

```
$ head -n 3 /etc/passwd | awk -F':' '{ print "User:", $1, " Shell:",
$7 }'
User: root  Shell: /bin/bash
User: daemon  Shell: /usr/sbin/nologin
User: bin  Shell: /usr/sbin/nologin
```

Here, -F':' tells awk to split fields based on the colon character.

awk can do incredibly complex data manipulation, report generation, and filtering. We've only scratched the surface here, but understanding its field-based processing and the basic pattern { action } structure unlocks enormous potential.

Putting Things in Order

Often, you'll need to arrange lines of text alphabetically, numerically, or based on specific columns. The sort command is designed for exactly this. It reads lines from files or standard input, sorts them according to specified criteria, and writes the result to standard output.

Basic Usage: By default, `sort` sorts lines alphabetically (lexicographically), considering the entire line.

```
$ cat celestial_bodies.txt | sort
Deimos
Earth
Jupiter
Mars
Mercury
Neptune
Our Moon
Phobos
Pluto (Dwarf Planet)
Saturn
Uranus
Venus
```

Key sort Options:

- -r (Reverse): Reverses the sorting order (e.g., Z to A).

```
$ sort -r celestial_bodies.txt
Venus
Uranus
Saturn
...
```

- -n (Numeric Sort): Sorts based on numeric value instead of alphabetical order. Crucial for sorting numbers correctly (otherwise "10" comes before "2").

```
$ # Create a file with numbers
$ printf "10\n2\n100\n5\n" > numbers.txt
$ sort numbers.txt # Alphabetical sort (incorrect for numbers)
10
100
2
5
$ sort -n numbers.txt # Numeric sort (correct)
2
5
10
100
```

- -k F (Key Field): Sorts based on a specific field (column) number F. Fields are assumed to be separated by whitespace by default.

- -t C (Field Separator): Specifies the character C that separates fields when using -k.

- -u (Unique): Outputs only the first line from a sequence of identical lines (based on the sort key). It's like running sort | uniq, but potentially more efficient.

Examples:

Let's use our data.txt file again.

```
$ # Sort data.txt numerically based on the second column
$ sort -k 2 -n data.txt
Item4   15    active
Item2   50    inactive
Item1   100   active
Item3   250   active

$ # Sort /etc/passwd by User ID (field 3), using ':' separator
$ head /etc/passwd | sort -t ':' -k 3 -n
root:x:0:0:root:/root:/bin/bash
daemon:x:1:1:daemon:/usr/sbin:/usr/sbin/nologin
bin:x:2:2:bin:/bin:/usr/sbin/nologin
sys:x:3:3:sys:/dev:/usr/sbin/nologin
sync:x:4:65534:sync:/bin:/bin/sync
...
```

sort is essential for organizing data before processing it further (especially with uniq) or simply for presenting information in a more logical order.

Counting Lines, Words, Characters

Need a quick count? The wc (word count) command tallies lines, words, and bytes (or characters) in its input.

Basic Usage:

```
$ wc celestial_bodies.txt
  9  11 114 celestial_bodies.txt
```

The output shows: 9 lines, 11 words, 114 bytes, followed by the filename. If reading from stdin, the filename isn't shown.

Key wc Options:

- -l (Lines): Count only the number of lines (newlines).
- -w (Words): Count only the number of words (sequences of non-whitespace characters).
- -c (Bytes): Count only the number of bytes.
- -m (Characters): Count characters (can differ from bytes for multi-byte character encodings like UTF-8).

Examples in Pipelines:

```
$ # Count files in the current directory
$ ls | wc -l
    10 # Example output

$ # Count how many processes are running as user 'jane'
$ ps aux | grep '^jane ' | wc -l
     5 # Example output
```

wc -l is particularly useful in pipelines for counting items or results.

Removing Duplicates

The uniq command is used to filter or report repeated lines. However, it has one crucial requirement: **it only detects adjacent duplicate lines**. This means you almost always need to sort the input *before* piping it to uniq.

Basic Usage:

```
$ # Create a file with duplicates
$ printf "apple\nbanana\norange\napple\nbanana\nbanana\n" > fruits.txt
$ cat fruits.txt
apple
banana
orange
apple
banana
banana

$ # Run uniq without sorting - ineffective
$ uniq fruits.txt
```

```
apple
banana
orange
apple
banana # Still shows duplicates because they weren't adjacent

$ # Sort first, then uniq - works!
$ sort fruits.txt | uniq
apple
banana
orange
```

Key uniq **Options:**

- -c (Count): Prefixes each output line with a count of how many times it occurred consecutively in the input.

  ```
  $ sort fruits.txt | uniq -c
        2 apple
        3 banana
        1 orange
  ```

- -d (Duplicates): Only prints lines that occurred more than once consecutively.

  ```
  $ sort fruits.txt | uniq -d
  apple
  banana
  ```

- -u (Unique): Only prints lines that occurred exactly once consecutively.

  ```
  $ sort fruits.txt | uniq -u
  orange
  ```

Remember the golden rule: sort before uniq for meaningful results across the whole input.

Translating Characters

The tr command is used to translate or delete characters. It reads from standard input and writes the modified text to standard output.

Basic Usage:

1. **Translating**: tr 'SET1' 'SET2' Replaces each character found in SET1 with the corresponding character in SET2. SET1 and SET2 are strings of characters.

```
$ # Convert lowercase to uppercase
$ echo "Hello World" | tr 'a-z' 'A-Z'
HELLO WORLD

$ # Simple substitution (Caesar cipher)
$ echo "HAL" | tr 'ABCDEFGHIJKLMNOPQRSTUVWXYZ'
'BCDEFGHIJKLMNOPQRSTUVWXYZA'
IBM
```

You can use character ranges like a-z, A-Z, 0-9 and special character classes like [:lower:], [:upper:], [:digit:], [:punct:], [:space:].

2. **Deleting**: tr -d 'SET' Deletes all characters found in SET.

```
$ # Delete all vowels (case-insensitive)
$ echo "Programming is fun" | tr -d 'aeiouAEIOU'
Prgrmmng s fn

$ # Delete all digits
$ echo "Order 123 for $45.67" | tr -d '[:digit:]'
Order  for $.
```

tr is great for simple character-level manipulations like case conversion or stripping specific character types.

Finding Differences

When you have two versions of a file (e.g., an original configuration file and one you modified), how do you see exactly what changed? The diff command compares two files line by line and reports the differences.

Basic Usage:

```
$ cp celestial_bodies.txt planets_v1.txt
$ # Make some changes to celestial_bodies.txt
$ sed -i 's/Mars/Red Planet/' celestial_bodies.txt
$ sed -i '/Pluto/d' celestial_bodies.txt # Delete the Pluto line
$ diff planets_v1.txt celestial_bodies.txt
4c4
< Mars
```

```
---
> Red Planet
9d8
< Pluto (Dwarf Planet)
```

Understanding the Default Output:

- NcM: Line number(s) N in file1 need to be changed (c), deleted (d), or added (a) relative to line number(s) M in file2.
- < line: A line from file1 that needs to be removed or changed.
- > line: A line from file2 that needs to be added or is part of a change.
- ---: Separator between lines from file1 and file2 in a change (c) block.

The default format is a bit cryptic. **Unified format (-u)** is much more common and easier to read:

```
$ diff -u planets_v1.txt celestial_bodies.txt
--- planets_v1.txt      2024-07-23 19:10:01.000000000 -0400
+++ celestial_bodies.txt        2024-07-23 19:10:30.000000000 -0400
@@ -1,11 +1,10 @@
 Mercury
 Venus
 Earth
-Mars
+Red Planet
 Jupiter
 Saturn
 Uranus
 Neptune
-Pluto (Dwarf Planet)
 Our Moon
 Phobos
 Deimos
```

Unified Format Explanation:

- --- file1 timestamp: Header line for the original file.
- +++ file2 timestamp: Header line for the new file.
- @@ -line1,count1 +line2,count2 @@: A "hunk" header, showing the line number and number of lines from each file covered by this chunk of differences.
- Lines prefixed with : Context lines (unchanged, shown for clarity).
- Lines prefixed with -: Lines present in file1 but *removed* in file2.

- Lines prefixed with +: Lines *added* in file2 that weren't in file1.

Other Key `diff` **Options:**

- `-i`: Ignore case differences.
- `-w`: Ignore changes in whitespace (spaces, tabs).
- `-r`: Recursively compare directories, showing differences in files within them.

`diff` (especially `diff -u`) is essential for code review, tracking configuration changes, and creating patches (files describing changes that can be applied using the `patch` command).

Extracting Columns

If you need to extract specific columns or character positions from lines, and `awk` seems like overkill, `cut` is a simpler alternative. It "cuts" out specified portions of each line.

Key Options:

- `-f FIELD_LIST` (Fields): Selects fields. Requires a delimiter (usually specified with -d). Fields are numbered starting from 1. `FIELD_LIST` can be a single number (`-f 1`), comma-separated (`-f 1,3`), or a range (`-f 2-4`).
- `-d DELIMITER` (Delimiter): Specifies the character separating fields when using `-f`. The default is the Tab character.
- `-c CHARACTER_LIST` (Characters): Selects specific character positions. Positions start from 1. `CHARACTER_LIST` can be single (`-c 1`), comma-separated (`-c 1,3,5`), or a range (`-c 1-10`).

Examples:

```
$ # Extract usernames (field 1) from /etc/passwd, using ':' delimiter
$ head -n 3 /etc/passwd | cut -d ':' -f 1
root
daemon
bin

$ # Extract username (field 1) and shell (field 7)
$ head -n 3 /etc/passwd | cut -d ':' -f 1,7
root:/bin/bash
daemon:/usr/sbin/nologin
bin:/usr/sbin/nologin

$ # Extract the first 10 characters of each line
```

```
$ cut -c 1-10 celestial_bodies.txt
Mercury
Venus
Earth
Red Planet
Jupiter
Saturn
Uranus
Neptune
Our Moon
Phobos
Deimos
```

cut is simple and efficient for extracting fixed-position or delimiter-separated columns when you don't need the advanced logic of awk.

Joining Files Line by Line

Finally, let's look at combining files.

paste

The paste command merges corresponding lines from multiple files, putting them side-by-side, separated by a Tab by default.

Let's create two files:

```
$ printf "Mercury\nVenus\nEarth\n" > planets_inner.txt
$ printf "Rocky\nHot\nHabitable\n" > planets_desc.txt

$ paste planets_inner.txt planets_desc.txt
Mercury Rocky
Venus   Hot
Earth   Habitable
```

- -d DELIMITER: Use a different delimiter instead of Tab. paste -d ',' file1 file2.

- -s (Serial): Concatenates lines from *one* file sequentially, separated by Tabs.

  ```
  $ paste -s planets_inner.txt
  Mercury     Venus     Earth
  ```

join

The `join` command is more sophisticated. It performs a relational database-style join on two files, combining lines that have an identical **join field** (the first field by default). **Important:** For `join` to work correctly, both input files usually need to be **sorted** based on the join field first!

Let's create two sorted files with a common ID:

```
$ printf "101:Alice\n102:Bob\n103:Charlie\n" | sort > names.txt
$ printf "101:Admin\n103:Dev\n104:QA\n" | sort > roles.txt

$ cat names.txt
101:Alice
102:Bob
103:Charlie
$ cat roles.txt
101:Admin
103:Dev
104:QA

$ # Join on the first field (default), use ':' as separator
$ join -t ':' names.txt roles.txt
101:Alice:Admin
103:Charlie:Dev
```

Notice that only lines with matching IDs (101 and 103) appear in the output. Bob (102) and QA (104) were excluded because they didn't have a match in the other file. `join` has many options (`-1 FIELD`, `-2 FIELD`, `-o FORMAT`) to control which fields to join on and how to format the output, making it powerful for combining related data sets.

Chapter Summary

This chapter armed you with a versatile arsenal of text-processing utilities. You learned to search for patterns with `grep`, perform stream editing (especially substitutions) with `sed`, and handle field-based data powerfully with `awk`. We covered organizing lines with `sort`, counting lines, words, and characters with `wc`, and removing adjacent duplicates from sorted input with `uniq`. You saw how to translate or delete characters using `tr`, compare files to find differences with `diff`, and extract specific columns or character positions with `cut`. Finally, we looked at combining files side-by-side with `paste` and merging them based on common fields with `join`.

These tools are the workhorses of command-line text manipulation. Individually use-ful, their true power emerges when combined in pipelines, allowing you to filter, transform, and analyze text data in countless ways. While powerful, remember that for highly complex parsing (like strict JSON or XML), dedicated tools or scripting might be better suited, but for the vast majority of text-based tasks on Linux, these utilities are indispensable.

Now that you can not only issue commands but also process their textual output effectively, you're ready for the next big step: writing your own commands! In Chapter 10, we will finally dive into the world of **shell scripting**, where you'll learn to combine these commands and shell features into reusable scripts to automate your tasks.

10

Writing Your First Script

You've come a long way! You can confidently navigate Linux, manage files and direct-ories, understand the critical permission system, wield powerful text-processing tools like those in Chapter 9, and even customize your shell environment (Chapter 8). You've learned to chain commands together with pipes and redirection (Chapter 6) to perform fairly complex tasks. But what if you need to perform that same sequence of commands repeatedly? Or what if the sequence is long and prone to typos? Typing everything out manually each time is inefficient and error-prone. It's time to take the next leap and automate your work by writing **shell scripts**. This chapter marks the beginning of your journey into scripting, where you'll learn how to bundle commands into reusable files, making you vastly more productive and unlocking the true poten-tial of the command line.

What is a Shell Script? Why Write Them?

At its heart, a shell script is incredibly simple: it's just a **plain text file containing a sequence of commands** that you would normally type at the shell prompt. Instead of typing them one by one, you put them into the file, and then you tell the shell (like Bash) to execute all the commands in that file, from top to bottom.

Think of it like writing down a recipe. Instead of remembering every step ("add flour," "add sugar," "mix") and performing them manually each time you want to bake a cake, you write the recipe down. Now, anyone (or any shell) can follow the recipe to get the same result consistently.

So, why bother writing scripts?

1. **Automation:** This is the biggest win. If you have a task involving multiple commands that you perform regularly (like backing up files, generating a report, cleaning up temporary directories), you can put those commands in a script and run the whole sequence with a single action. This saves enormous amounts of time and effort.

2. **Consistency:** Scripts ensure that tasks are performed exactly the same way every single time. This eliminates errors caused by typos or forgotten steps when executing commands manually.

3. **Efficiency:** Running one script is much faster than typing many commands individually, especially complex ones.

4. **Customization:** You can essentially build your own custom commands tailored to your specific needs by combining existing Linux utilities in novel ways within a script.

5. **Sharing:** You can easily share your scripts with colleagues or the wider community, allowing others to benefit from your automated workflows.

Shell scripting bridges the gap between using individual commands and full-blown programming, providing a powerful way to automate system administration, development tasks, data processing, and much more.

Creating a Script File

Let's create our very first script file. As mentioned, it's just a text file. You can use any text editor you like. We introduced `nano` and `vim` in Chapter 4; `nano` is often easier for beginners.

Navigate to your `playground` directory (`cd ~/playground`) where we can experiment safely. Let's create a file for our script. It's common practice to give shell script files a `.sh` extension, although Linux doesn't strictly require it. The extension helps humans (and sometimes other tools) identify the file as a shell script. Good filenames are usually descriptive, lowercase, and might use underscores to separate words.

```
$ cd ~/playground
$ nano first_script.sh
```

This opens the nano editor, ready for you to type your script commands.

The Shebang Line Explained

The very first line of almost every shell script you write should be what's known as the **shebang** (or sometimes "hashbang"). It looks like this:

```
#!/bin/bash
```

Let's break this down:

- `#`: Normally, the hash symbol indicates a comment in shell scripts (as we'll see shortly).
- `!`: However, when `#!` appears as the *very first two characters* of a file, it has a special meaning to the Linux kernel.
- `/bin/bash`: This is the absolute path to the program (the **interpreter**) that should be used to execute the rest of the commands in this file.

Essentially, the shebang line tells the system: "When someone tries to run this file directly as an executable, don't try to run it yourself; instead, hand the whole file over to the `/bin/bash` program and let *it* handle the execution."

Since this book focuses on Bash scripting, `#!/bin/bash` is the shebang you'll use most often. However, you might encounter scripts using other interpreters:

- `#!/bin/sh`: Use the standard POSIX-compliant shell (often a simpler version of Bash or a different shell entirely like `dash`). Scripts written for `/bin/sh` tend to be more portable across different UNIX-like systems but might lack some Bash-specific features.
- `#!/usr/bin/env python3`: For a Python 3 script.
- `#!/usr/bin/perl`: For a Perl script.

For our purposes, **always start your Bash scripts with** `#!/bin/bash`. It ensures your script is interpreted by the Bash shell we're learning about, even if the user running it has a different default shell.

So, in your `nano` editor, type this as the very first line of `first_script.sh`:

```
#!/bin/bash
```

Now, let's add some actual commands below the shebang line.

Adding Comments

Before we add commands, let's talk about comments. Any line in a shell script that begins with a hash symbol (#), *except* for the shebang line, is treated as a **comment**. The shell completely ignores comments when executing the script.

Why use comments?

- **Explain** *Why*: Describe the purpose of a tricky command or a specific section of the script.
- **Explain** *How*: Clarify complex logic or non-obvious steps.
- **Metadata**: Include information like author, date created, usage instructions.
- **Debugging**: Temporarily "comment out" lines of code to disable them without deleting them.

Good commenting makes your scripts understandable, both to others and to your future self when you revisit the script months later!

Let's add some comments to our script in nano:

```
#!/bin/bash
# My first shell script
# Author: Your Name
# Date: July 23, 2024
#
# This script demonstrates basic commands and comments.
```

Running Basic Commands Within a Script

Now for the main event: adding Linux commands that will actually *do* something. Let's add a few simple commands we already know to our `first_script.sh` file below the comments.

```
#!/bin/bash
# My first shell script
# Author: Your Name
# Date: July 23, 2024
#
# This script demonstrates basic commands and comments.

echo "Starting my first script!" # Print a starting message
```

```
echo "My current location is:"
pwd # Show the present working directory

echo "The contents of this directory are:"
ls # List the files

echo "Script finished." # Print an ending message
```

Make sure the commands are typed exactly as you would at the prompt. Now, save the file and exit nano (press Ctrl+O, then Enter, then Ctrl+X).

You've written your first script! But how do you run it?

Executing Your Script

There are two primary ways to execute the commands contained in your first_script.sh file.

Method 1: Using the Shell Directly

You can explicitly tell the bash interpreter to read and execute the commands in your script file by passing the script's filename as an argument to bash:

```
$ bash first_script.sh
Starting my first script!
My current location is:
/home/jane/playground
The contents of this directory are:
Archive                mydata.txt           playground_contents.txt
celestial_bodies.txt   myscript.sh          planets_backup.txt
combined_log.log       Notes                planets_inner.txt
data.txt               planets.txt          planets_v1.txt
find_errors.log        planets_desc.txt     PrivateStuff
first_script.sh        playground_list.log  TextFiles
LogsBackup
Script finished.
```

How it works:

- You run the bash program.
- bash reads the first_script.sh file line by line.
- It ignores comments and the shebang line (since *it* is already Bash).

- It executes each command (echo, pwd, ls, echo) just as if you had typed them interactively.

Notice that for this method, the script file **does not need execute permission.** bash just needs permission to *read* the file. This is a quick way to run a script, especially one you just wrote or downloaded.

Method 2: Making it Executable

The more conventional way to run a script, especially one you intend to use like a regular command, is to make it directly executable. This involves two steps:

1. **Add Execute Permission:** As we learned in Chapter 5, files need execute permission (x) for the system to allow them to be run as programs. We use the chmod command for this. The +x option adds execute permission for the user (owner), group, and others, which is usually sufficient.

```
$ ls -l first_script.sh # Check permissions before
-rw-r--r-- 1 jane jane 229 Jul 23 20:15 first_script.sh
$ chmod +x first_script.sh
$ ls -l first_script.sh # Check permissions after
-rwxr-xr-x 1 jane jane 229 Jul 23 20:15 first_script.sh
```

See the x characters that appeared in the permissions string? Now the system knows it *can* be executed.

2. **Run the Script:** Now that it has execute permission, you might think you can just type first_script.sh. Try it:

```
$ first_script.sh
bash: first_script.sh: command not found...
```

Why didn't that work? Remember the $PATH variable from Chapter 8? The shell only looks for commands in the directories listed in $PATH. For security reasons, the **current directory (.) is typically not included in the** $PATH. If it were, someone could place a malicious script named ls in a directory, trick you into running it, and cause harm.

To run an executable file that's in your current directory but not in your $PATH, you must tell the shell *exactly* where it is by providing a **path** to it. The path to the current directory is represented by a single dot (.). So, you need to run it like this:

```
$ ./first_script.sh
Starting my first script!
My current location is:
/home/jane/playground
The contents of this directory are:
Archive                mydata.txt           playground_contents.txt
celestial_bodies.txt   myscript.sh          planets_backup.txt
combined_log.log       Notes                planets_inner.txt
data.txt               planets.txt          planets_v1.txt
find_errors.log        planets_desc.txt     PrivateStuff
first_script.sh        playground_list.log  TextFiles
LogsBackup
Script finished.
```

How it works:

- You tell the shell to execute the file located at `./first_script.sh` (the file `first_script.sh` in the current directory `.`).
- The kernel sees the file has execute permission.
- It looks at the very first line and sees the shebang `#!/bin/bash`.
- The kernel invokes the `/bin/bash` interpreter.
- `/bin/bash` then reads the rest of the `first_script.sh` file and executes the commands within it.

The `./` prefix is essential when running executables (including scripts) located in the current directory. If you moved the script to a directory that *is* in your `$PATH` (like `~/bin` if you created one and added it to `$PATH`), then you could run it just by typing `first_script.sh`.

Making a script executable (`chmod +x`) and running it with `./script_name` is the standard way to treat your scripts like custom commands.

A Slightly More Complex Example

Let's create another script, `organize_notes.sh`, that does a little more work: creates a dated directory inside `Notes` and moves a hypothetical `draft_notes.txt` file into it.

```
$ nano organize_notes.sh
```

Add the following content:

```
#!/bin/bash
```

```
# organize_notes.sh - Creates a dated subdirectory in Notes
# and moves draft_notes.txt into it.

echo "Starting note organization..."

# Define the main notes directory (using a variable!)
NOTES_DIR="$HOME/playground/Notes"
DRAFT_FILE="$HOME/playground/draft_notes.txt" # Assuming this file exists

# Create a directory name based on the current date (YYYY-MM-DD)
# We use command substitution $(...) here - more in Chapter 11!
TODAYS_DATE=$(date +%Y-%m-%d)
TARGET_DIR="$NOTES_DIR/$TODAYS_DATE"

echo "Target directory will be: $TARGET_DIR"

# Create the target directory, -p ensures parent dirs exist if needed
# and doesn't complain if the dir already exists.
mkdir -p "$TARGET_DIR"
echo "Created (or ensured existence of) $TARGET_DIR"

# Check if the draft file actually exists before trying to move it
if [ -f "$DRAFT_FILE" ]; then
  echo "Moving $DRAFT_FILE to $TARGET_DIR..."
  mv "$DRAFT_FILE" "$TARGET_DIR/"
else
  echo "Warning: $DRAFT_FILE not found. Nothing to move."
fi

echo "Note organization finished."
```

Save and exit nano. Now, make it executable and run it:

```
$ touch draft_notes.txt # Create the dummy file to be moved
$ chmod +x organize_notes.sh
$ ./organize_notes.sh
Starting note organization...
Target directory will be: /home/jane/playground/Notes/2024-07-23
Created (or ensured existence of) /home/jane/playground/Notes/2024-07-23
Moving /home/jane/playground/draft_notes.txt to
/home/jane/playground/Notes/2024-07-23...
Note organization finished.

$ ls Notes/ # Check the Notes directory
2024-07-23  important_notes.txt
$ ls Notes/2024-07-23/ # Check the new subdirectory
```

This script uses variables, command substitution ($(...)), and even a simple if statement (we'll cover these properly soon!) to perform a more useful task. It demonstrates how you can start combining commands and shell features to build real tools.

Chapter Summary

Congratulations! You've officially become a shell scripter. In this chapter, you learned that a **shell script** is simply a text file containing commands, designed for **automation**, **consistency**, and **efficiency**. You saw how to create a script file and the critical importance of the **shebang** line (#!/bin/bash) to specify the correct interpreter. We covered the two main ways to execute scripts: explicitly using the interpreter (bash script.sh) or making the script **executable** (chmod +x script.sh) and running it via its path (./script.sh), understanding why the ./ is usually necessary. You also learned the value of adding **comments** (#) for readability and maintainability. We created and ran a basic script and then a slightly more involved example, hinting at the power that comes from combining commands within a script structure.

You now know the mechanics of creating and running simple scripts. But our current scripts are static; they do the same thing every time. To make them truly dynamic and interactive, we need to introduce variables for storing changing data, learn how to capture user input, and understand how the shell handles quoting and expansion. In the next chapter, we'll dive into using variables within scripts and reading input from the user, making your scripts much more flexible and powerful.

11
Using Variables and Reading Input

In the previous chapter, you took the exciting step of writing your first shell scripts, learning how to bundle commands into executable files. Our initial scripts were simple, executing the same sequence of commands every time. But the real power of scripting comes when you make them dynamic – able to handle different data, respond to changing conditions, or interact with the user. The key to this dynamism lies in **variables** and **input/output**. This chapter delves deeper into using variables effectively *within* your scripts, exploring the crucial concept of quoting, capturing the output of commands into variables, performing basic arithmetic, and learning how to make your scripts interactive by reading input directly from the user or from arguments passed on the command line.

Defining and Using Variables in Scripts

We briefly touched on variables in Chapter 8 when customizing the environment, and even used one in our `organize_notes.sh` script. Now, let's formalize their use within scripts.

As you saw, defining a variable is straightforward:

```
variable_name=value
```

Remember the rules:

- No spaces around the equals sign (=).
- Variable names typically use letters, numbers, and underscores, starting with a letter.
- Names are case-sensitive (`FILENAME` is different from `filename`). Conventionally, user-defined variables are often lowercase or `snake_case`, while environment variables inherited from the system are often uppercase (`UPPER_CASE`).

To use the value stored in a variable, you prepend its name with a dollar sign ($). This tells the shell to **substitute** the variable name with its value before executing the command line. This is often called **variable expansion**.

Let's create a script, `variable_demo.sh`, to illustrate:

```
nano variable_demo.sh
```

Add the following content:

```
#!/bin/bash
# variable_demo.sh - Demonstrates defining and using variables

# Define some variables
user_name="Alice"
user_city="Wonderland"
file_count=5

# Use the variables in echo commands
echo "Processing data for user: $user_name"
echo "$user_name lives in $user_city."
echo "Found $file_count files for $user_name."

# Using braces for clarity or concatenation
echo "Files belong to ${user_name}_data" # Braces needed here!
echo "Next count will be $file_count+1" # Prints literally $file_count+1

# Variable reassignment
file_count=10
echo "Updated file count: $file_count"
```

Save the script (Ctrl+O, Enter), make it executable (chmod +x variable_demo.sh), and run it (./variable_demo.sh):

```
$ ./variable_demo.sh
Processing data for user: Alice
Alice lives in Wonderland.
Found 5 files for Alice.
Files belong to Alice_data
Next count will be 5+1
Updated file count: 10
```

Key Observations:

- The shell replaced $user_name, $user_city, and $file_count with their assigned values ("Alice", "Wonderland", 5).
- In ${user_name}_data, the curly braces {} were necessary to clearly separate the variable name (user_name) from the literal text (_data) immediately following it. Without the braces, the shell would look for a variable named user_name_data, which doesn't exist. Braces are good practice whenever a variable is immediately followed by text that could be part of a valid variable name.
- echo "Next count will be $file_count+1" printed the literal string 5+1. Variable expansion happened, but the +1 was just treated as text. We'll see how to perform actual arithmetic shortly.
- Variables can be reassigned new values later in the script.

Understanding Variable Scope

As mentioned in Chapter 8, variables defined within a script are **local** to that script's execution context by default. They are not automatically visible to other scripts or commands that your script might call, unless you explicitly export them.

Consider script_a.sh:

```bash
#!/bin/bash
# script_a.sh
local_var="I am in Script A"
export exported_var="Also from Script A, but exported"

echo "[Script A] Local var: $local_var"
echo "[Script A] Exported var: $exported_var"
```

```
echo "[Script A] Calling Script B..."
# Assuming script_b.sh is in the same directory and executable
./script_b.sh
```

And `script_b.sh`:

```
#!/bin/bash
# script_b.sh
echo "[Script B] Trying to access local_var: $local_var"
echo "[Script B] Trying to access exported_var: $exported_var"
```

Make both executable (`chmod +x script_a.sh script_b.sh`) and run `script_a.sh`:

```
$ ./script_a.sh
[Script A] Local var: I am in Script A
[Script A] Exported var: Also from Script A, but exported
[Script A] Calling Script B...
[Script B] Trying to access local_var:   # <-- It's empty!
[Script B] Trying to access exported_var: Also from Script A, but exported
```

As expected, `script_b.sh` could only see `exported_var` because it was explicitly exported by `script_a.sh`. The `local_var` was confined to `script_a.sh`. We'll explore scope further when we discuss functions in Chapter 14. For now, remember that simple assignments create local variables, and `export` makes them environment variables for child processes.

Quoting Matters

How you enclose strings containing variables makes a big difference. This is one of the most common sources of confusion for new scripters.

- **Double Quotes ("...")**: **Weak Quoting**
    - Preserves most literal characters within the quotes.
    - Allows **variable expansion** (`$var`), **command substitution** (`$(...)` or `` `` ``), and **arithmetic expansion** (`$((...))`).
    - Special characters like `$` (for variables), `\` (escape), and `` ` `` (backtick for command substitution) retain their special meaning.
- **Single Quotes ('...')**: **Strong Quoting**
    - Preserves the **literal value** of *every* character within the quotes.

- **No** variable expansion, command substitution, or arithmetic expansion occurs. Everything is treated as plain text.
- **Backticks (`` `command` ``): Legacy Command Substitution**
  - This is the older syntax for command substitution (see next section). It's generally **discouraged** in favor of $(...) because it's harder to read and nest.

Let's see the difference:

```bash
#!/bin/bash
# quoting_demo.sh

the_user="Bob"
the_command="pwd"

echo "Double Quotes:"
echo "User: $the_user, Command output: $($the_command), Math: $((10+5))"

echo "" # Empty line for separation

echo "Single Quotes:"
echo 'User: $the_user, Command output: $($the_command), Math: $((10+5))'

echo ""

echo "Backticks (Legacy):"
echo "User: $the_user, Command output: `$the_command`"
```

Run it:

```
$ ./quoting_demo.sh
Double Quotes:
User: Bob, Command output: /home/jane/playground, Math: 15

Single Quotes:
User: $the_user, Command output: $($the_command), Math: $((10+5))

Backticks (Legacy):
User: Bob, Command output: /home/jane/playground
```

Analysis:

- **Double Quotes:** Correctly substituted $the_user, executed the command stored in $the_command using $($the_command), and performed the arithmetic $((10+5)).
- **Single Quotes:** Printed everything literally, including $the_user, $($the_command), and $((10+5)). No expansion or execution happened.
- **Backticks:** Worked for command substitution, but $() is preferred.

Rule of Thumb:

- Use **double quotes** by default when you need variable expansion or command substitution within a string.
- Use **single quotes** when you want to represent a string exactly as written, with no shell interpretation.
- Always quote your variables (echo "$my_var") unless you specifically *know* you need the shell to perform word splitting or filename expansion on the value (advanced cases). Quoting prevents unexpected behavior if the variable's value contains spaces or special characters.

Command Substitution

We saw a glimpse of this in the quoting examples and organize_notes.sh. Often, you need to capture the output of a command and store it in a variable for later use in your script. This is called **command substitution**.

The modern and preferred syntax is $(command). The shell executes command inside the parentheses, captures its standard output, and substitutes that output back into the command line.

```bash
#!/bin/bash
# cmd_subst_demo.sh

echo "Using command substitution:"

# Get the current date and time
current_datetime=$(date +"%Y-%m-%d %H:%M:%S")
echo "Current time: $current_datetime"

# Get the number of files in the current directory
num_files=$(ls | wc -l)
echo "Number of files here: $num_files"

# Get the kernel version
kernel_ver=$(uname -r)
```

```
echo "Kernel version: $kernel_ver"

# Use the result in further commands
echo "Creating log file named kernel_${kernel_ver}.log"
touch "kernel_${kernel_ver}.log"
ls kernel*.log
```

Run it:

```
$ ./cmd_subst_demo.sh
Using command substitution:
Current time: 2024-07-23 21:10:45
Number of files here:        18
Kernel version: 5.15.0-78-generic
Creating log file named kernel_5.15.0-78-generic.log
kernel_5.15.0-78-generic.log
```

Command substitution is incredibly powerful. It allows you to dynamically generate filenames, process lists of files, get system information, and much more, integrating the output of any command directly into your script's logic. Remember to use the $ (...) syntax.

Arithmetic Expansion

What about that echo "Next count will be $file_count+1" example that didn't work? To perform arithmetic calculations in the shell, you need **arithmetic expansion**, using the $((expression)) syntax.

The shell evaluates the mathematical expression inside the double parentheses and substitutes the result.

```
#!/bin/bash
# arithmetic_demo.sh

num1=50
num2=15

# Basic operations
sum=$((num1 + num2))
difference=$((num1 - num2))
product=$((num1 * num2)) # Asterisk usually needs quoting/escaping in shell
quotient=$((num1 / num2)) # Integer division
remainder=$((num1 % num2)) # Modulo
```

```
echo "$num1 + $num2 = $sum"
echo "$num1 - $num2 = $difference"
echo "$num1 * $num2 = $product"
echo "$num1 / $num2 = $quotient (integer division)"
echo "$num1 % $num2 = $remainder"

# Incrementing a variable
counter=0
echo "Initial counter: $counter"
counter=$((counter + 1)) # Add 1
echo "After increment: $counter"

# Shorter increment syntax (like C)
((counter++)) # Note: No '$' needed inside ((...)) for variables
echo "After ((counter++)): $counter"

# Comparison within ((...)) returns 1 for true, 0 for false.
# Useful in conditional contexts (Chapter 12)
echo "Is $num1 > $num2 ? Result: $((num1 > num2)) (1 means true)"
```

Run it:

```
$ ./arithmetic_demo.sh
50 + 15 = 65
50 - 15 = 35
50 * 15 = 750
50 / 15 = 3 (integer division)
50 % 15 = 5
Initial counter: 0
After increment: 1
After ((counter++)): 2
Is 50 > 15 ? Result: 1 (1 means true)
```

(Note: The C-style $((...))$ without the leading $ can also be used for arithmetic evaluation and assignment, especially increments/decrements, but $((...))$ is needed for substitution into strings/commands).

Bash arithmetic only handles **integers**. For floating-point calculations, you typically need to use external utilities like bc or awk.

```
$ num1=10
$ num2=3
$ # Using bc for floating point division
$ result=$(echo "scale=4; $num1 / $num2" | bc)
```

```
$ echo "$num1 / $num2 = $result"
10 / 3 = 3.3333
```

Getting Data from the User

So far, our variables have been hardcoded in the script. To make scripts truly interactive, you often need to ask the user for input. The built-in read command is used for this. It reads a single line from standard input (usually the keyboard) and assigns it to one or more variables.

Basic Syntax:

```
read variable_name
```

Let's try an interactive script ask_user.sh:

```
#!/bin/bash
# ask_user.sh - Gets input from the user

echo "Hello! What is your name?"
read user_name # Reads input until Enter, stores in user_name

echo "And what city do you live in?"
read user_city

echo "Nice to meet you, $user_name from $user_city!"
```

Run it:

```
$ ./ask_user.sh
Hello! What is your name?
Alice # <-- Typed by user
And what city do you live in?
Wonderland # <-- Typed by user
Nice to meet you, Alice from Wonderland!
```

Useful read Options:

- -p PROMPT (Prompt): Displays the PROMPT string on the same line, without a trailing newline, before waiting for input. This is usually cleaner than using a separate echo.

```
#!/bin/bash
# read_prompt.sh
read -p "Enter your username: " username
read -sp "Enter your password: " password # -s makes input silent
echo # Print a newline after silent password input
echo "Thank you, $username."
```

- -s (Silent): Does not echo the user's input to the screen. Ideal for passwords.

- -t TIMEOUT (Timeout): Waits only TIMEOUT seconds for input before failing.

- Reading multiple variables: read var1 var2 var3 ... reads the line and splits it into words (based on whitespace), assigning consecutive words to var1, var2, etc. The last variable gets the rest of the line.

```
#!/bin/bash
# read_multi.sh
read -p "Enter first name, last name, age: " fname lname age
echo "Name: $fname $lname, Age: $age"
```

Run it:

```
$ ./read_multi.sh
Enter first name, last name, age: Bob Smith 42
Name: Bob Smith, Age: 42
```

The read command is fundamental for creating interactive scripts that adapt based on user responses.

Command Line Arguments

Another way to pass information *into* a script without interactive prompts is through **command line arguments**. These are the extra words you type after the script name when you run it.

Inside the script, these arguments are available through special positional parameters:

- $0: The name of the script itself.
- $1: The first argument after the script name.
- $2: The second argument.
- $3: The third argument, and so on...
- $9: The ninth argument.

- ${10}, ${11}, ...: For arguments beyond the 9th, you need curly braces.

Other special variables related to arguments:

- $#: The **number** of arguments passed to the script (not counting $0).
- $*: All arguments presented as a **single string**, joined by the first character of the IFS (Internal Field Separator) variable (usually a space). "$*" treats all arguments as one word.
- $@: All arguments presented as **separate strings**. "$@" treats each argument as a distinct, quoted word. This is generally the **safest and most useful** way to refer to all arguments, especially if they contain spaces.

Let's create show_args.sh:

```
#!/bin/bash
# show_args.sh - Displays command line arguments

echo "Script name (\$0): $0"
echo "Number of arguments (\$#): $#"
echo "First argument (\$1): $1"
echo "Second argument (\$2): $2"
echo "Third argument (\$3): $3"

echo ""
echo "All args as single string (\$*): $*"
echo "All args as separate strings (\$@): $@"

echo ""
echo "Looping through args using \"\$@\":"
for arg in "$@"
do
  echo "  Argument: $arg"
done
```

Make it executable and run it with some arguments, including one with spaces:

```
$ ./show_args.sh hello world "third arg with spaces" 123
Script name ($0): ./show_args.sh
Number of arguments ($#): 4
First argument ($1): hello
Second argument ($2): world
Third argument ($3): third arg with spaces

All args as single string ($*): hello world third arg with spaces 123
All args as separate strings ($@): hello world third arg with spaces 123
```

```
Looping through args using "$@":
  Argument: hello
  Argument: world
  Argument: third arg with spaces
  Argument: 123
```

Command line arguments allow you to create flexible scripts that operate on different files or with different options each time they are run, without requiring interactive input. For example, `cp $1 $2` could be a simple script to copy the file specified by the first argument to the name given by the second argument.

Chapter Summary

This chapter significantly boosted your scripting capabilities. You learned how to effectively define and use **variables** within scripts for storing data and the importance of **variable scope** (local vs. exported environment variables). We untangled the critical differences between **single quotes** (literal) and **double quotes** (expansion allowed) and why quoting variables (`"$var"`) is usually essential. You discovered how to capture the output of commands using **command substitution** `$()` and perform integer math using **arithmetic expansion** `$((...))`. We made scripts interactive by reading user input with the `read` command and its useful options like `-p` (prompt) and `-s` (silent). Finally, you learned how to access data passed to the script via **command line arguments** using positional parameters (`$1`, `$2`, …), the argument count (`$#`), and the special `$*` and `$@` variables (preferring `"$@"` for most use cases).

Your scripts can now handle dynamic data, perform calculations, and interact with users or command-line input. The next logical step is to add decision-making capabilities. How can a script choose different actions based on user input, the existence of a file, or the result of a command? Chapter 12 introduces conditional logic using `if`, `else`, and `case` statements, allowing your scripts to branch and adapt intelligently.

12

Making Decisions

In the last chapter, we infused our scripts with dynamism using variables, command substitution, and user input (both interactive via `read` and through command-line arguments like $1). Your scripts can now handle changing data. But what if you need the script to *react* differently based on that data? What if it should only perform an action if a file exists, or if the user enters a specific value, or if a command succeeds? To achieve this, scripts need the ability to make decisions, to follow different paths based on certain conditions. This chapter introduces the fundamental concepts of **conditional logic** in Bash scripting. We'll explore the `if` statement, learn how to test various conditions using `test` and the modern `[[ ... ]]` construct, and see how to handle multiple possibilities with `else`, `elif`, and the versatile `case` statement. Get ready to teach your scripts how to think!

The `if` Statement

The most fundamental conditional construct is the `if` statement. Its basic job is to execute a block of commands *only if* a specific condition is true.

The simplest structure looks like this:

```
if <condition_command>
then
  # Commands to execute if the condition is true
  command1
```

```
  command2
  ...
fi # Marks the end of the if block
```

How it works:

1. The shell executes the `<condition_command>`.
2. It then checks the **exit status** of that command. Remember from Chapter 7 that commands report success or failure via an exit status code (stored briefly in $?). An exit status of **zero (0)** conventionally means **success** (or "true" in a logical sense), while any **non-zero** exit status means **failure** (or "false").
3. If the `<condition_command>` exits with a status of **0 (true)**, the shell executes the commands between `then` and `fi`.
4. If the `<condition_command>` exits with a **non-zero status (false)**, the shell skips all the commands between `then` and `fi` and continues execution after the `fi`.

The `fi` keyword (`if` spelled backward) is essential to mark the end of the `if` statement's block.

What kind of `<condition_command>` can we use? Literally *any* command that produces an exit status! A common example is using `grep` to check if a pattern exists:

```
#!/bin/bash
# if_grep_demo.sh

FILENAME="planets.txt"
PATTERN="Earth"

echo "Checking if '$PATTERN' exists in '$FILENAME'..."

# grep -q makes grep quiet (no output), it just sets the exit status.
# 0 if found (true), non-zero if not found (false).
if grep -q "$PATTERN" "$FILENAME"
then
  echo "'$PATTERN' was found in the file!"
fi

# Check for a pattern that doesn't exist
if grep -q "Krypton" "$FILENAME"
then
  echo "'Krypton' was found in the file! (This shouldn't print)"
fi

echo "Script finished."
```

Make it executable (chmod +x if_grep_demo.sh) and run it:

```
$ ./if_grep_demo.sh
Checking if 'Earth' exists in 'planets.txt'...
'Earth' was found in the file!
Script finished.
```

The first if block executed because grep -q "Earth" planets.txt succeeded (found the pattern, exit status 0). The second if block was skipped because grep -q "Krypton" planets.txt failed (pattern not found, non-zero exit status).

While using commands like grep directly works, it's more common to use dedicated test commands for typical conditions like checking files or comparing values.

Testing Conditions

Instead of relying solely on the exit status of general commands, Bash provides a built-in command specifically designed for evaluating conditions within if statements: the test command.

You can write:

```
if test -f "$FILENAME"
then
  echo "$FILENAME exists and is a regular file."
fi
```

However, test has a very common alternative syntax using square brackets [...]. The following is *exactly equivalent* to the command above:

```
if [ -f "$FILENAME" ] # Note the mandatory spaces after [ and before ]
then
  echo "$FILENAME exists and is a regular file."
fi
```

The opening bracket [is actually just another name for the test command! The closing bracket] is simply required as the last argument when using the [form. **Crucially, you must have spaces** immediately after the opening [and immediately before the closing]. Think of [as a command name, and like any command, it needs to be separated from its arguments by spaces.

The `test` command (and its `[` alias) provides numerous operators to perform different kinds of checks:

File Tests

These operators check various attributes of files or directories. Remember `$FILENAME` should be properly quoted if it might contain spaces!

Operator	True If...	Example
`-e file`	file exists (any type)	`[ -e "$FILENAME" ]`
`-f file`	file exists and is a regular file	`[ -f "$FILENAME" ]`
`-d file`	file exists and is a directory	`[ -d "$DIRNAME" ]`
`-r file`	file exists and is readable by you	`[ -r "$FILENAME" ]`
`-w file`	file exists and is writable by you	`[ -w "$FILENAME" ]`
`-x file`	file exists and is executable by you	`[ -x "$SCRIPTNAME" ]`
`-s file`	file exists and has a size greater than zero	`[ -s "$DATAFILE" ]`
`-O file`	file exists and is Owned by your effective user ID	`[ -O "$FILENAME" ]`
`-G file`	file exists and its Group matches your effective group ID	`[ -G "$FILENAME" ]`

Example Script (`file_test_demo.sh`):

```bash
#!/bin/bash
# file_test_demo.sh

FILE_TO_CHECK="planets.txt"
DIR_TO_CHECK="Notes"
NON_EXISTENT="no_such_file"

echo "Checking '$FILE_TO_CHECK'..."
if [ -e "$FILE_TO_CHECK" ]
then
  echo "  Exists (-e)"
  if [ -f "$FILE_TO_CHECK" ]
  then
    echo "  Is a regular file (-f)"
  fi
  if [ -s "$FILE_TO_CHECK" ]
  then
    echo "  Is not empty (-s)"
  fi
else
  echo "  Does NOT exist (-e)" # We'll add 'else' formally soon
fi
```

```
echo "Checking '$DIR_TO_CHECK'..."
if [ -d "$DIR_TO_CHECK" ]
then
  echo "  Is a directory (-d)"
fi

echo "Checking '$NON_EXISTENT'..."
if [ ! -e "$NON_EXISTENT" ] # '!' negates the test
then
  echo "  Does NOT exist (! -e)"
fi
```

Run it:

```
$ ./file_test_demo.sh
Checking 'planets.txt'...
  Exists (-e)
  Is a regular file (-f)
  Is not empty (-s)
Checking 'Notes'...
  Is a directory (-d)
Checking 'no_such_file'...
  Does NOT exist (! -e)
```

(Note: The ! operator negates the result of the test that follows it).

String Comparisons

These operators compare text strings. **It is vital to double-quote your variables** when doing string comparisons to prevent errors if the variable is empty or contains spaces.

Operator	True If...	Example
string1 = string2	string1 is **equal** to string2	["$ANSWER" = "yes"]
string1 == string2	Also **equal** (more readable, Bash extension)	["$USER" == "root"]
string1 != string2	string1 is **not equal** to string2	["$STATUS" != "done"]
-z string	string has zero length (is empty)	[-z "$ERROR_MSG"]
-n string	string has non-zero length (is not empty)	[-n "$USER_INPUT"]

Example Script (string_test_demo.sh):

```
#!/bin/bash
```

```
# string_test_demo.sh

name1="Alice"
name2="Bob"
empty_string=""

if [ "$name1" = "Alice" ]
then
  echo "'$name1' is equal to 'Alice'"
fi

if [ "$name1" != "$name2" ]
then
  echo "'$name1' is not equal to '$name2'"
fi

if [ -z "$empty_string" ]
then
  echo "empty_string is empty (-z)"
fi

if [ -n "$name1" ]
then
  echo "'$name1' is not empty (-n)"
fi

# Importance of quoting
tricky_var="Contains  spaces"
# if [ $tricky_var = "Contains  spaces" ] # This might fail!
# then ... fi
if [ "$tricky_var" = "Contains  spaces" ] # This works reliably
then
  echo "Quoted comparison with spaces worked."
fi
```

Run it:

```
$ ./string_test_demo.sh
'Alice' is equal to 'Alice'
'Alice' is not equal to 'Bob'
empty_string is empty (-z)
'Alice' is not empty (-n)
Quoted comparison with spaces worked.
```

Integer Comparisons

These operators compare whole numbers (integers).

Operator	True If...	Example
int1 -eq int2	int1 is equal to int2	["$COUNT" -eq 0]
int1 -ne int2	int1 is not equal to int2	["$?" -ne 0]
int1 -gt int2	int1 is greater than int2	["$LINES" -gt 100]
int1 -ge int2	int1 is greater than or equal to int2	["$AGE" -ge 18]
int1 -lt int2	int1 is less than int2	["$TEMP" -lt 0]
int1 -le int2	int1 is less than or equal to int2	["$ERRORS" -le 5]

Example Script (integer_test_demo.sh):

```bash
#!/bin/bash
# integer_test_demo.sh

count=10
limit=20
errors=0

if [ "$count" -lt "$limit" ]
then
  echo "$count is less than $limit"
fi

if [ "$errors" -eq 0 ]
then
  echo "There are no errors."
fi


# Get number of arguments from Chapter 11
if [ "$#" -ge 1 ] # Check if at least one argument was passed
then
  echo "Received $# arguments."
else
  echo "No arguments received."
fi
```

Run it (first without, then with arguments):

```
$ ./integer_test_demo.sh
10 is less than 20
There are no errors.
```

```
No arguments received.

$ ./integer_test_demo.sh arg1 arg2
10 is less than 20
There are no errors.
Received 2 arguments.
```

While [is portable and widely used, it has some quirks related to word splitting and filename expansion, especially if you forget to quote variables. For Bash scripting, there's often a better way.

The Modern Test

Bash provides an enhanced conditional construct called the **compound command** [[...]]. It looks similar to [...] but behaves more intuitively and offers more features directly within Bash, often eliminating the need for the external `test` command and its associated quoting pitfalls.

Key Advantages of [[...]]:

1. **No Word Splitting/Filename Expansion:** Variables used within [[...]] are generally safe from unexpected word splitting or filename expansion, even if unquoted (though quoting is still good practice for clarity and consistency).
2. **Built-in Logical Operators:** You can use && (AND) and || (OR) directly *inside* the double brackets, making compound conditions much cleaner than the older -a and -o operators used with [.
3. **Pattern Matching:** Includes the =~ operator for matching against extended regular expressions (covered in Chapter 16).
4. **Lexicographical Comparison:** Uses < and > for string comparison based on current locale settings (inside [[...]] only).

Recommendation: When writing scripts specifically for Bash (which we are in this book), **prefer using** [[...]] **over** [...] for most conditional tests. It's generally safer and more powerful.

Let's rewrite some previous examples using [[...]]:

```
#!/bin/bash
# double_bracket_demo.sh

FILENAME="planets.txt"
```

```
tricky_var="Contains  spaces"
count=10
limit=20

# File test (same syntax)
if [[ -f "$FILENAME" ]]
then
  echo "[[]]: '$FILENAME' is a file."
fi

# String test (quoting often optional but recommended)
if [[ $tricky_var == "Contains  spaces" ]] # '==' is preferred in [[
then
  echo "[[]]: String comparison worked (even with spaces)."
fi

# Integer test (same syntax)
if [[ "$count" -lt "$limit" ]]
then
  echo "[[]]: $count is less than $limit."
fi

# Combined test using &&
if [[ -f "$FILENAME" && "$count" -lt "$limit" ]]
then
  echo "[[]]: File exists AND count is less than limit."
fi
```

Run it:

```
$ ./double_bracket_demo.sh
[[]]: 'planets.txt' is a file.
[[]]: String comparison worked (even with spaces).
[[]]: 10 is less than 20.
[[]]: File exists AND count is less than limit.
```

The syntax for the tests themselves (-f, -eq, ==, etc.) is largely the same, but the surrounding [[...]] provides a more robust context in Bash.

Branching Out

The basic if statement executes commands only if the condition is true. What if you want to execute one set of commands if true, and a *different* set if false? That's what the else clause is for.

if-else **Structure**

```
if <condition_command>
then
   # Commands if condition is TRUE
   command_A1
   command_A2
else
   # Commands if condition is FALSE
   command_B1
   command_B2
fi
```

Example (check_user.sh):

```
#!/bin/bash
# check_user.sh

TARGET_USER="root"

# Using [[ ... ]]
if [[ "$USER" == "$TARGET_USER" ]]
then
   echo "You are running as the '$TARGET_USER' user. Be careful!"
else
   echo "You are running as user '$USER'."
fi
```

Run it (once as your normal user, once using sudo if possible):

```
$ ./check_user.sh
You are running as user 'jane'.

$ sudo ./check_user.sh
You are running as the 'root' user. Be careful!
```

if-elif-else **Structure**

What if you have more than two possibilities? You can check multiple conditions sequentially using elif (short for "else if").

```
if <condition1>
then
```

```
  # Commands if condition1 is TRUE
  commands_A
elif <condition2>
then
  # Commands if condition1 is FALSE and condition2 is TRUE
  commands_B
elif <condition3>
then
  # Commands if condition1 & 2 are FALSE and condition3 is TRUE
  commands_C
else
  # Commands if ALL preceding conditions are FALSE
  commands_D
fi
```

The shell evaluates the conditions in order. As soon as it finds one that is true, it executes the corresponding `then` block and then skips straight to the `fi`. The final `else` block (which is optional) catches any cases where none of the preceding `if` or `elif` conditions were true.

Example (`file_type_checker.sh` using arguments from Chapter 11):

```
#!/bin/bash
# file_type_checker.sh

# Check if exactly one argument was provided
if [[ "$#" -ne 1 ]]
then
  echo "Usage: $0 <file_or_directory_path>"
  exit 1 # Exit script with an error status
fi

ITEM="$1" # Assign the first argument to a variable

if [[ ! -e "$ITEM" ]]
then
  echo "Error: '$ITEM' does not exist."
  exit 2
elif [[ -f "$ITEM" ]]
then
  echo "'$ITEM' is a regular file."
elif [[ -d "$ITEM" ]]
then
  echo "'$ITEM' is a directory."
else
  echo "'$ITEM' exists but is neither a regular file nor a directory."
```

```
fi

exit 0 # Explicitly exit with success status
```

Run it with different inputs:

```
$ ./file_type_checker.sh planets.txt
'planets.txt' is a regular file.
$ ./file_type_checker.sh Notes/
'Notes/' is a directory.
$ ./file_type_checker.sh /dev/tty # Example of 'other' type
'/dev/tty' exists but is neither a regular file nor a directory.
$ ./file_type_checker.sh no_such_thing
Error: 'no_such_thing' does not exist.
$ ./file_type_checker.sh # No arguments
Usage: ./file_type_checker.sh <file_or_directory_path>
```

(Note the use of exit 1 *and* exit 2 *to signal different error conditions, and* exit 0 *for success. This is good practice).*

Combining Tests

Often, you need to check if multiple conditions are true (AND) or if at least one of several conditions is true (OR).

- **Inside** [[...]]: Use && for AND, || for OR.

    ```
    file="data.txt"
    size=$(wc -c < "$file") # Command substitution

    if [[ -r "$file" && "$size" -gt 1024 ]]
    then
       echo "$file is readable AND larger than 1KB."
    fi

    read -p "Continue? (y/n): " answer
    if [[ "$answer" == "y" || "$answer" == "Y" ]]
    then
       echo "Proceeding..."
    fi
    ```

- **Inside [...]**: Use -a for AND, -o for OR. These are generally **less preferred** than && and || inside [[...]] because they have tricky precedence rules and can be less readable.

```
# Less preferred syntax:
if [ -r "$file" -a "$size" -gt 1024 ]
then ... fi

if [ "$answer" = "y" -o "$answer" = "Y" ]
then ... fi
```

- **Negation**: Use ! to negate a test (works in both [and [[).

```
if [[ ! -w "$file" ]]
then
  echo "$file is NOT writable."
fi
```

Choosing from Many Options

When you need to check a variable against several specific, distinct values (patterns), using nested if-elif-else statements can become cumbersome. The case statement provides a cleaner alternative for this scenario.

Structure:

```
case "$variable" in
  pattern1)
    # Commands if variable matches pattern1
    commands_A
    ;; # Terminator for this block
  pattern2|pattern3) # Use | for OR within a pattern
    # Commands if variable matches pattern2 OR pattern3
    commands_B
    ;;
  pattern*) # Patterns can include wildcards like * or ?
    # Commands if variable matches pattern*
    commands_C
    ;;
  *) # Default case (matches anything not matched above)
    # Commands for the default case
    commands_D
    ;;
```

```
esac # Marks the end of the case block ('case' spelled backward)
```

How it works:

1. The value of $variable is compared against each `pattern` in order.
2. The *first* pattern that matches is selected.
3. The commands associated with that matching pattern (up to the double semi-colon ; ;) are executed.
4. Execution then jumps directly to `esac`. Only one block of commands is ever executed.
5. The *) pattern acts as a default catch-all if no other patterns match.
6. Patterns can use shell wildcards (*, ?, []).

Example (`simple_menu.sh`):

```bash
#!/bin/bash
# simple_menu.sh

echo "Simple Menu:"
echo "  a) List files"
echo "  b) Show current date"
echo "  c) Check disk usage"
echo "  q) Quit"

read -p "Enter your choice: " choice

echo # Add a blank line

case "$choice" in
  a|A) # Match lowercase 'a' or uppercase 'A'
    echo "Listing files in current directory:"
    ls -l
    ;;
  b|B)
    echo "Current date and time:"
    date
    ;;
  c|C)
    echo "Disk usage (filesystem root):"
    df -h /
    ;;
  q|Q)
    echo "Quitting."
    ;;
  *) # Default case for invalid input
```

```
      echo "Invalid choice '$choice'."
      ;;
 esac


 echo "Done."
```

Run it and try different options:

```
$ ./simple_menu.sh
Simple Menu:
  a) List files
  b) Show current date
  c) Check disk usage
  q) Quit
Enter your choice: b

Current date and time:
Tue Jul 23 22:15:30 EDT 2024
Done.

$ ./simple_menu.sh
Simple Menu:
  ...
Enter your choice: x

Invalid choice 'x'.
Done.
```

The case statement is particularly useful for processing command-line options or handling responses with a limited set of expected values.

Chapter Summary

This chapter empowered your scripts with decision-making capabilities. You learned the fundamental if...then...fi structure and how it relies on command **exit status**. We explored the traditional test command and its bracketed alias [...], covering essential **file tests** (-f, -d, -e, etc.), **string comparisons** (=, !=, -z, -n), and **integer comparisons** (-eq, -ne, -gt, etc.). We then introduced the more robust and recommended Bash **compound command** [[...]], highlighting its advantages for variable handling and built-in logical operators (&&, ||). You learned how to create branches using if-else and multi-way branches with if-elif-else. Finally, we saw how the `case...esac` statement provides an elegant way to handle situations where a variable needs to be checked against multiple specific patterns.

Your scripts can now analyze situations and react accordingly. But what about performing actions repeatedly? Many automation tasks involve processing multiple files, reading data line by line, or simply doing something a fixed number of times. For that, we need loops. In the next chapter, we'll explore Bash's looping constructs: `for`, `while`, and `until`.

13

Repeating Yourself

In the previous chapter, you gave your scripts the power of decision-making using conditional logic like `if` and `case`. They can now react differently based on conditions. But what about tasks that require doing something *over and over* again? Imagine needing to rename a hundred files, process every line in a configuration file, or check a system status every minute until a certain condition is met. Doing this manually is tedious, and even writing individual commands in a script for each repetition is impractical. This is where **loops** come into play. Loops allow you to execute a block of commands repeatedly, either a fixed number of times, for each item in a list, or as long as (or until) a certain condition holds true. Mastering loops is fundamental to automation and writing efficient shell scripts. Let's explore the three main looping constructs in Bash: `for`, `while`, and `until`.

The `for` Loop

The `for` loop is ideal when you have a known set of items – like a list of filenames, usernames, or server names – and you want to perform the same action(s) for each item in that set.

Basic `for` Loop Structure

The most common form iterates over a list of words (strings separated by spaces or newlines).

```
for variable_name in item1 item2 item3 ...
do
  # Commands to execute for each item
  # Use $variable_name to access the current item
  command1 "$variable_name"
  command2
  ...
done # Marks the end of the loop
```

How it works:

1. The shell looks at the list of items provided after the in keyword.
2. In the first iteration, it assigns the first item (item1) to the variable_name.
3. It then executes the commands between do and done. Inside this block, you can use $variable_name to refer to the current item (item1).
4. When it reaches done, the shell loops back. It assigns the *next* item (item2) to variable_name and executes the commands again.
5. This continues until all items in the list have been processed.
6. Execution then continues with the command immediately following done.

Example: Looping through strings

```
#!/bin/bash
# for_string_demo.sh

echo "Looping through planets:"
for planet in Mercury Venus Earth Mars Jupiter Saturn Uranus Neptune
do
  echo "  Processing planet: $planet"
  # Imagine doing something more complex with each planet name here
done

echo "Loop finished."
```

Make it executable (chmod +x for_string_demo.sh) and run it:

```
$ ./for_string_demo.sh
Looping through planets:
  Processing planet: Mercury
  Processing planet: Venus
  Processing planet: Earth
  Processing planet: Mars
  Processing planet: Jupiter
  Processing planet: Saturn
```

```
    Processing planet: Uranus
    Processing planet: Neptune
Loop finished.
```

Looping Through Filenames (Using Wildcards)

A very common use case for for loops is to process multiple files matching a certain pattern. You can use the shell's wildcard expansion (globbing, remember Chapter 3) directly in the in list.

```
#!/bin/bash
# for_files_demo.sh

# Create some dummy files for demonstration
echo "Creating test files..."
touch file_a.txt file_b.log script.sh image.jpg data_1.csv data_2.csv
ls

echo ""
echo "Processing only .txt files:"
# The shell expands *.txt into a list of matching filenames
for txt_file in *.txt
do
  # Check if the item found is actually a file (prevents issues if no .txt files
exist)
  if [[ -f "$txt_file" ]]; then
    echo "  Found text file: $txt_file"
    echo "    -> First line:"
    head -n 1 "$txt_file" # Print first line (will be empty for these files)
  fi
done

echo ""
echo "Cleaning up test files..."
rm file_a.txt file_b.log script.sh image.jpg data_1.csv data_2.csv

echo "File loop finished."
```

Run it:

```
$ ./for_files_demo.sh
Creating test files...
Archive                file_b.log             playground_contents.txt
celestial_bodies.txt   first_script.sh        planets_backup.txt
```

```
combined_log.log      image.jpg           planets_desc.txt
data_1.csv            kernel_...log       planets_inner.txt
data_2.csv            LogsBackup          planets.txt
data.txt              mydata.txt          planets_v1.txt
file_a.txt            myscript.sh         PrivateStuff
find_errors.log       Notes               TextFiles
# ... other files ...

Processing only .txt files:
  Found text file: celestial_bodies.txt
    -> First line:
Mercury
  Found text file: data.txt
    -> First line:
Item1   100   active
  Found text file: file_a.txt
    -> First line:

  Found text file: mydata.txt
    -> First line:

  Found text file: planets_backup.txt
    -> First line:
Mercury
  Found text file: planets_desc.txt
    -> First line:
Rocky
  Found text file: planets_inner.txt
    -> First line:
Mercury
  Found text file: planets.txt
    -> First line:
Mercury
  Found text file: planets_v1.txt
    -> First line:
Mercury
  Found text file: playground_contents.txt
    -> First line:
total 20

Cleaning up test files...
File loop finished.
```

The *.txt was expanded by the shell into a list of all filenames ending in .txt in the current directory, and the loop processed each one. The if [[-f "$txt_file"]] check is important; if no `.txt` files existed, the loop might otherwise run once with the literal string `*.txt` as the value, leading to errors.

Looping Through Command Substitution Output

You can dynamically generate the list of items using command substitution (`$(...)`, Chapter 11).

```
#!/bin/bash
# for_command_demo.sh

# Get a list of directories in /etc
# NOTE: This is fragile if directory names contain spaces or newlines!
# See 'while read' later for a safer way to process 'find' output.
echo "Directories in /etc (using simple command substitution):"
for dir_name in $(find /etc -maxdepth 1 -type d -print)
do
  echo "  Found directory: $dir_name"
done
```

Run it (output will vary):

```
$ ./for_command_demo.sh
Directories in /etc (using simple command substitution):
  Found directory: /etc
  Found directory: /etc/default
  Found directory: /etc/network
  Found directory: /etc/X11
  Found directory: /etc/apt
  ...
```

Caution: Using command substitution like this relies on the shell splitting the command's output based on whitespace (spaces, tabs, newlines). This can break if filenames or the items themselves contain spaces. We'll see a more robust method using `while read` later in this chapter.

C-Style `for` Loops

Bash also supports a `for` loop syntax similar to the C programming language, which is useful for loops that need to run a specific number of times based on a counter.

Syntax:

```
for (( initializer; condition; update_step ))
do
  # Commands to execute
  ...
done
```

- initializer: An expression executed once before the loop starts (e.g., i=0).
- condition: An arithmetic expression evaluated before each iteration. If it evaluates to true (non-zero in arithmetic context, confusingly!), the loop body executes. If false (zero), the loop terminates.
- update_step: An expression executed at the end of each iteration (e.g., i++ to increment i).

Example:

```
#!/bin/bash
# for_c_style_demo.sh

echo "Counting from 1 to 5:"
for (( count=1; count<=5; count++ ))
do
  echo "  Current count is: $count"
done

echo ""
echo "Counting down from 3 to 0:"
for (( i=3; i>=0; i-- ))
do
  echo "  Launch sequence: T-$i"
done
echo "Liftoff!"
```

Run it:

```
$ ./for_c_style_demo.sh
Counting from 1 to 5:
  Current count is: 1
  Current count is: 2
  Current count is: 3
  Current count is: 4
  Current count is: 5

Counting down from 3 to 0:
  Launch sequence: T-3
```

```
    Launch sequence: T-2
    Launch sequence: T-1
    Launch sequence: T-0
 Liftoff!
```

Note that inside the double parentheses ((...)), you don't need the $ prefix for variables (e.g., count++ not $count++), similar to arithmetic expansion $((...)) as seen in Chapter 11. This C-style loop is very handy for purely numerical iterations.

The while **Loop**

While the for loop iterates over a fixed list, the while loop executes a block of commands *as long as* a specified condition remains true. It checks the condition *before* each iteration.

Structure:

```
while <condition_command>
do
  # Commands to execute while the condition is TRUE (exit status 0)
  command1
  command2
  ...
done # Marks the end of the loop
```

How it works:

1. The shell executes the <condition_command>.
2. It checks the exit status. If it's **0 (true)**, the commands between do and done are executed.
3. When done is reached, execution loops back to step 1 to re-evaluate the condition.
4. If the <condition_command> exits with a **non-zero status (false)**, the loop terminates immediately, and execution continues after done.

Classic Counter Loop Example:

We can simulate the C-style for loop using while:

```
#!/bin/bash
# while_counter_demo.sh
```

```
counter=1
limit=5

echo "While loop from 1 to $limit:"

# Using [[ ... ]] for the condition (Chapter 12)
while [[ "$counter" -le "$limit" ]]
do
   echo "  Count: $counter"
   # Manually increment the counter inside the loop
   ((counter++))
done

echo "Loop finished. Counter is now: $counter"
```

Run it:

```
$ ./while_counter_demo.sh
While loop from 1 to 5:
   Count: 1
   Count: 2
   Count: 3
   Count: 4
   Count: 5
Loop finished. Counter is now: 6
```

It's crucial to have something *inside* the loop that eventually makes the condition false (like ((counter++))), otherwise you'll create an infinite loop!

Reading Files Line by Line

This is one of the most important and robust uses of the while loop: processing a file line by line, correctly handling spaces and other special characters within lines.

The standard idiom looks like this:

```
while IFS= read -r line
do
   # Process the variable "$line" which contains the current line
   echo "Processing line: $line"
done < input_file.txt
```

Let's break down this critical construct:

- `while ... done < input_file.txt`: This is crucial. Input redirection (`<`) is applied to the *entire* `while` loop. This means the `read` command inside the loop reads directly from the opened file, one line per iteration.
- `read -r line`: The `read` command (Chapter 11) reads one line of input.
  - `-r`: Prevents backslash (`\`) interpretation, ensuring lines are read literally. Essential for handling file paths or data containing backslashes.
  - `line`: The variable where the entire line's content will be stored.
- `IFS=`: This is subtle but important. `IFS` (Internal Field Separator) is a shell variable that determines how `read` splits words (by default, space, tab, newline). Setting `IFS=` immediately before `read` (making it local to that command) prevents `read` from trimming leading/trailing whitespace from the line. If you want `read` to split the line into multiple variables based on whitespace or another delimiter, you would omit `IFS=` or set it differently (e.g., `IFS=','` `read col1 col2 ...`).
- The `while` loop continues as long as the `read` command successfully reads a line. `read` returns a non-zero exit status (false) when it reaches the end of the file, causing the loop to terminate.

Example: Processing `planets.txt` safely

```bash
#!/bin/bash
# while_read_demo.sh

INPUT_FILE="planets.txt"
line_num=0

echo "Processing '$INPUT_FILE' line by line:"

if [[ ! -f "$INPUT_FILE" ]]; then
  echo "Error: Input file '$INPUT_FILE' not found."
  exit 1
fi

while IFS= read -r current_line
do
  ((line_num++))
  echo "  Line $line_num: ->$current_line<-"
done < "$INPUT_FILE"

echo "Finished processing $line_num lines."
```

Run it:

```
$ ./while_read_demo.sh
Processing 'planets.txt' line by line:
   Line 1: ->Mercury<-
   Line 2: ->Venus<-
   Line 3: ->Earth<-
   Line 4: ->Red Planet<- # Assuming change from previous chapter
   Line 5: ->Jupiter<-
   Line 6: ->Saturn<-
   Line 7: ->Uranus<-
   Line 8: ->Neptune<-
   Line 9: ->Our Moon<- # Assuming Pluto was deleted
   Line 10: ->Phobos<-
   Line 11: ->Deimos<-
Finished processing 11 lines.
```

Why is `< file while read` **preferred over** `cat file | while read`? When you use a pipe (`cat file | while read ...`), the `while` loop often runs in a **subshell**. This means any variables created or modified *inside* that `while` loop (like `line_num` in our example if we didn't initialize it outside) will disappear once the loop finishes, as the subshell exits. Redirecting input to the loop (`while read ... done < file`) avoids creating this subshell, so variable changes persist after the loop.

Infinite Loops

Sometimes you genuinely want a loop to run forever (or until explicitly stopped, perhaps with `Ctrl+C` or a `break` statement inside). The `true` command always exits with status 0 (success).

```
#!/bin/bash
# infinite_demo.sh

count=0
# 'true' always succeeds, so the loop condition is always met
while true
do
  echo "Loop iteration: $((++count)) - Time: $(date +%T)"
  sleep 2 # Pause for 2 seconds
done
```

Run this script, and it will print the message every two seconds indefinitely. You'll need to press `Ctrl+C` to stop it. Such loops are often used for monitoring tasks or simple background services.

The until Loop

The until loop is the logical opposite of the while loop. It executes a block of commands *as long as* a specified condition is **false** (returns a non-zero exit status). It checks the condition *before* each iteration.

Structure:

```
until <condition_command>
do
  # Commands to execute while the condition is FALSE (non-zero exit status)
  command1
  command2
  ...
done # Marks the end of the loop
```

How it works:

1. The shell executes the <condition_command>.
2. It checks the exit status. If it's **non-zero (false)**, the commands between do and done are executed.
3. When done is reached, execution loops back to step 1 to re-evaluate the condition.
4. If the <condition_command> exits with a status of **0 (true)**, the loop terminates immediately, and execution continues after done.

Example: Waiting for a file to exist

```
#!/bin/bash
# until_demo.sh

TARGET_FILE="signal.go"

echo "Waiting for file '$TARGET_FILE' to appear..."

# Loop UNTIL the file exists (-e returns 0/true when it exists)
until [[ -e "$TARGET_FILE" ]]
do
  echo "File not found yet ($(date +%T)). Waiting 5 seconds..."
  sleep 5
done

echo ""
echo "File '$TARGET_FILE' has appeared! Proceeding..."
```

```
# rm "$TARGET_FILE" # Optional cleanup
```

To test this, run `./until_demo.sh` in one terminal. Then, in *another* terminal, navigate to the same playground directory and create the file (`touch signal.go`). You'll see the first terminal detect the file and exit the loop.

`until` is less common than `while` because most conditions are naturally phrased in a positive sense ("while this is true..."), but it's useful when the logic fits better with waiting for a condition to *stop* being false.

Controlling Loop Execution

Sometimes, you need finer control over your loops than just letting them run until the main condition fails. You might need to exit the loop early or skip the rest of the current iteration.

break: Exiting a Loop Early

The `break` command immediately terminates the **innermost** loop it's contained within (whether `for`, `while`, or `until`). Execution jumps straight to the command following the done statement of that loop.

Use Case: Stop processing a file once a specific condition is met.

```
#!/bin/bash
# break_demo.sh

INPUT_FILE="celestial_bodies.txt"
STOP_WORD="Saturn"
count=0

echo "Searching for '$STOP_WORD' in '$INPUT_FILE'..."

while IFS= read -r line
do
  ((count++))
  echo "Line $count: $line"
  if [[ "$line" == "$STOP_WORD" ]]
  then
    echo "Found '$STOP_WORD'! Stopping the loop."
    break # Exit the while loop immediately
  fi
  # This part only runs if the 'if' condition was false
```

167

```
    echo "  (Still searching...)"
done < "$INPUT_FILE"

echo "Loop finished after processing $count lines."
```

Run it:

```
$ ./break_demo.sh
Searching for 'Saturn' in 'celestial_bodies.txt'...
Line 1: Mercury
  (Still searching...)
Line 2: Venus
  (Still searching...)
Line 3: Earth
  (Still searching...)
Line 4: Red Planet
  (Still searching...)
Line 5: Jupiter
  (Still searching...)
Line 6: Saturn
Found 'Saturn'! Stopping the loop.
Loop finished after processing 6 lines.
```

continue: Skipping to the Next Iteration

The continue command skips the remaining commands *within the current iteration* of the innermost loop and jumps directly to the *next* iteration (re-evaluating the loop condition for while/until, or getting the next item for for).

Use Case: Skipping comment lines or blank lines when processing a file.

```
#!/bin/bash
# continue_demo.sh

# Create a dummy config file
printf "user=alice\n# Database settings\ndb_host=localhost\n\nport=3306\n" >
config.conf

echo "Processing config.conf, skipping comments and blank lines:"

while IFS= read -r line
do
  # Skip blank lines
  if [[ -z "$line" ]]; then
```

```
      # echo "  (Skipping blank line)" # Uncomment for debugging
      continue # Go to next iteration (read next line)
   fi

   # Skip comment lines (lines starting with #)
   # Note: Using [[ $line == \#* ]] pattern matching
   if [[ "$line" == \#* ]]; then
      # echo "  (Skipping comment: $line)" # Uncomment for debugging
      continue # Go to next iteration
   fi

   # If we reach here, it's a valid line
   echo "  Valid setting: $line"
done < config.conf

echo "Finished processing config file."
rm config.conf # Cleanup
```

Run it:

```
$ ./continue_demo.sh
Processing config.conf, skipping comments and blank lines:
  Valid setting: user=alice
  Valid setting: db_host=localhost
  Valid setting: port=3306
Finished processing config file.
```

Nested Loops and `break n`/`continue n`

If you have loops inside other loops (nested loops), `break` and `continue` normally only affect the loop they are immediately inside. If you need to break out of multiple levels of loops or continue an outer loop from an inner one, you can optionally provide a number n (`break n` or `continue n`) to specify how many enclosing loops to break out of or continue. Using deeply nested loops and `break n`/`continue n` can often make scripts harder to understand, so use this feature sparingly. Often, restructuring the logic or using functions (Chapter 14) is a clearer approach.

Chapter Summary

This chapter introduced the essential concept of repetition in shell scripting through loops. You learned about the versatile **for loop**, perfect for iterating over lists of items, filenames (using wildcards), command output, or using the C-style syntax for numerical counting. We explored the condition-driven `while` **loop**, which repeats as long as a condition is true, and mastered the crucial `while read` idiom for safely processing files line by line. You also met the `until` **loop**, which repeats as long as a condition is false. Finally, you gained finer control over loop execution using `break` to exit a loop prematurely and `continue` to skip to the next iteration.

Loops are the backbone of automation in shell scripting, allowing you to perform repetitive tasks efficiently and process large amounts of data systematically. With conditionals (Chapter 12) and loops now in your toolkit, your scripts can exhibit quite complex behavior. However, as scripts grow, organizing the code becomes increasingly important. In the next chapter, we'll introduce **functions**, a way to group related commands into reusable blocks, making your scripts more modular, readable, and maintainable.

14

Organizing Code with Functions

As your scripts grow beyond simple sequences of commands, incorporating the variables, input handling, conditional logic (Chapter 12), and loops (Chapter 13) we've discussed, they can start to become long and difficult to manage. You might find yourself repeating the same block of code in multiple places, or a single script might try to do too many different things, making it hard to read and debug. Just like organizing physical tools in a workshop makes tasks easier, organizing code within your scripts is crucial for maintainability. This chapter introduces **functions**, a fundamental programming concept that allows you to group related commands under a single name, creating reusable, modular blocks of code within your scripts. Learning to use functions effectively will make your scripts cleaner, more organized, and much easier to work with.

Why Use Functions?

Imagine you're building something complex, perhaps assembling furniture. You have several distinct steps: attaching legs, fixing the back panel, installing shelves. Instead of having one giant instruction sheet listing every single screw turn, it's often clearer to have separate instructions for each sub-task: "Assemble Leg Unit," "Attach Back Panel," etc. Functions in shell scripting serve a similar purpose.

Here's why they are so beneficial:

1. **Modularity:** Functions allow you to break down a large script into smaller, logical, self-contained units. Each function performs a specific, well-defined task. This makes the overall script structure much easier to understand.

2. **Reusability (DRY - Don't Repeat Yourself):** If you need to perform the same sequence of commands multiple times within your script, you can put those commands into a function and then simply "call" that function whenever needed. This avoids duplicating code, making your script shorter and reducing the chance of errors (if you need to fix a bug, you only fix it in one place – the function).

3. **Readability:** By giving meaningful names to blocks of code (the function names), you make your script read more like a series of high-level steps rather than a dense sequence of low-level commands. This improves clarity significantly.

4. **Maintainability & Debugging:** When code is modularized into functions, it's easier to test and debug individual parts. If something goes wrong, you can often isolate the problem to a specific function. Changes or updates to a particular piece of logic only need to happen within the relevant function.

Using functions is a hallmark of well-structured programming, even in shell scripts.

Defining a Simple Function

There are two common syntaxes for defining a function in Bash:

Syntax 1 (Preferred):

```
function_name() {
  # Commands that make up the function body
  command1
  command2
  ...
  # Optional 'return' statement (more on this later)
}
```

Syntax 2 (Older, KornShell compatible):

```
function function_name {
  # Commands that make up the function body
  command1
  command2
```

```
    ...
}
```

The first syntax, `function_name() { ... }`, is generally preferred in modern Bash scripting as it's more visually distinct and closer to function definitions in other programming languages. We will use this syntax throughout the book.

Let's define a very simple function in a script called `function_hello.sh`:

```bash
#!/bin/bash
# function_hello.sh - Basic function definition and call

# --- Function Definition ---
# This function prints a simple greeting.
greet_user() {
    echo "--------------------"
    echo "Hello there, user!"
    echo "Welcome to the script."
    echo "--------------------"
}
# --- End of Function Definition ---

# --- Main script execution starts here ---
echo "Script starting..."

# Call the function
greet_user

echo "Script finished."
# --- End of main script ---
```

Key Points:

- The function definition (`greet_user() { ... }`) just defines *what* the function does; it **does not execute** the commands inside it yet.
- The commands inside the curly braces { ... } form the **function body**.
- You typically define your functions near the top of your script, before the main part of the script that calls them (though Bash is flexible about this).

Calling a Function

Once a function is defined, how do you execute the commands inside it? You simply use the function's name as if it were a regular command.

Look back at `function_hello.sh`. The line `greet_user` in the main part of the script is the **function call**. When the shell encounters this line, it finds the definition of the `greet_user` function and executes the commands within its body.

Let's make the script executable (`chmod +x function_hello.sh`) and run it:

```
$ ./function_hello.sh
Script starting...
--------------------
Hello there, user!
Welcome to the script.
--------------------
Script finished.
```

You see the output from the echo commands *inside* the `greet_user` function appeared exactly where the function was called in the main script flow. You can call the same function multiple times:

```
#!/bin/bash
# function_multi_call.sh

greet_user() {
   echo ">>>>> Entering Greeting Function <<<<<"
}

echo "Before first call."
greet_user
echo "Between calls."
greet_user
echo "After second call."
```

Run it (`chmod +x function_multi_call.sh && ./function_multi_call.sh`):

```
$ ./function_multi_call.sh
Before first call.
>>>>> Entering Greeting Function <<<<<
Between calls.
>>>>> Entering Greeting Function <<<<<
After second call.
```

Each call executes the function's body independently. This demonstrates the reusability aspect.

Passing Arguments to Functions

Just like scripts can accept command-line arguments (Chapter 11), functions can accept arguments passed to them when they are called. Inside the function, these arguments are accessed using the same positional parameters we saw before, but they are **local to the function's execution**:

- $1, $2, $3, ...: The first, second, third, etc., argument passed to the function.
- $0: Remains the name of the script itself (not the function name).
- $#: The number of arguments passed to the *function*.
- $*, $@, "$@": Represent all arguments passed to the *function* (remember "$@" is usually preferred).

Let's create a function that takes arguments:

```bash
#!/bin/bash
# function_args.sh

# Function definition: Takes a name and a city as arguments
print_location_info() {
  # Check if the correct number of arguments were passed *to the function*
  if [[ "$#" -ne 2 ]]; then
    echo "Usage Error (inside function): print_location_info <name> <city>"
    # We'll discuss 'return' properly soon
    return 1 # Indicate an error occurred within the function
  fi

  local person_name="$1" # Assign arguments to descriptive local variables
  local person_city="$2"

  echo "Function received:"
  echo "  Name: $person_name"
  echo "  City: $person_city"
  echo "  Number of args to function: $#"
}

# Main script
echo "Calling function with arguments..."
print_location_info "Alice" "Wonderland" # Call with 2 arguments

echo ""
echo "Calling function with different arguments..."
print_location_info "Bob" # Call with only 1 argument (will trigger error)

echo ""
```

```
echo "Script finished."
```

Run it (chmod +x function_args.sh && ./function_args.sh):

```
$ ./function_args.sh
Calling function with arguments...
Function received:
  Name: Alice
  City: Wonderland
  Number of args to function: 2

Calling function with different arguments...
Usage Error (inside function): print_location_info <name> <city>

Script finished.
```

Observations:

- Inside `print_location_info`, `$1` referred to "Alice" in the first call and "Bob" in the second. `$2` was "Wonderland" in the first call, but empty in the second.
- `$#` inside the function correctly reported the number of arguments passed *to that specific function call*.
- The `if` check inside the function validated the number of arguments passed to the function itself.

Using arguments makes functions much more flexible, allowing them to operate on different data provided at the time they are called. Using descriptive local variables (like `person_name`) for `$1`, `$2` etc., inside the function improves readability.

Returning Values from Functions

Functions, like any command or script, finish with an **exit status** (0 for success, non-zero for failure). This is the primary way a function signals *whether it succeeded or failed*. However, sometimes you want a function to compute a value or produce some data that the main script can then use. There are two main ways functions "return" information:

Method 1: Exit Status (`return`)

The `return` command is used *inside* a function to explicitly set its exit status and immediately stop the function's execution.

Syntax:

```
return N # Where N is an integer between 0 and 255
```

- `return 0`: Signals success (conventional).
- `return 1` (or any non-zero value up to 255): Signals failure. Different non-zero values can optionally be used to indicate different types of errors.

If a function finishes without an explicit `return` statement, its exit status is the exit status of the *last command executed* within the function body.

The caller (the main script) can check the function's exit status using $? immediately after the function call, or more commonly, directly within an `if` statement.

```bash
#!/bin/bash
# function_return_status.sh

# Function checks if a file exists and is non-empty
check_file() {
  local filename="$1"
  echo "Checking file: $filename"

  if [[ ! -e "$filename" ]]; then
    echo "Error: File does not exist."
    return 1 # Error code 1: Not found
  fi

  if [[ ! -s "$filename" ]]; then
    echo "Error: File exists but is empty."
    return 2 # Error code 2: Empty file
  fi

  # If we reach here, checks passed
  echo "File is valid."
  return 0 # Success
}

# Main script
echo "--- Test 1: Valid file ---"
if check_file "planets.txt"; then # Checks if exit status is 0
  echo "Check succeeded!"
else
  echo "Check failed! Exit status: $?"
fi

echo ""
```

```
echo "--- Test 2: Non-existent file ---"
if check_file "no_such_file.txt"; then
  echo "Check succeeded!"
else
  echo "Check failed! Exit status: $?"
fi

echo ""
echo "--- Test 3: Empty file ---"
touch empty_test_file.txt
if check_file "empty_test_file.txt"; then
  echo "Check succeeded!"
else
  echo "Check failed! Exit status: $?"
fi
rm empty_test_file.txt # Cleanup
```

Run it:

```
$ ./function_return_status.sh
--- Test 1: Valid file ---
Checking file: planets.txt
File is valid.
Check succeeded!

--- Test 2: Non-existent file ---
Checking file: no_such_file.txt
Error: File does not exist.
Check failed! Exit status: 1

--- Test 3: Empty file ---
Checking file: empty_test_file.txt
Error: File exists but is empty.
Check failed! Exit status: 2
```

Using `return` with exit statuses is the standard way for functions to indicate success or failure, just like regular Linux commands.

Method 2: Standard Output

What if you need a function to "return" actual data, like a calculated number or a processed string, not just a success/failure code? The most common shell idiom for this is to have the function **print the desired result to its standard output** (`stdout`) and have the caller capture that output using **command substitution** (`$(...)`).

```bash
#!/bin/bash
# function_return_data.sh

# Function calculates the sum of two numbers
calculate_sum() {
  local num1=$1
  local num2=$2
  local sum=$((num1 + num2))
  echo "$sum" # Print the result to stdout
  # Implicitly returns exit status 0 (success) because 'echo' succeeded
}

# Function gets the first word of a string
get_first_word() {
  local input_string="$1"
  # Use cut to get the first field (word)
  echo "$input_string" | cut -d ' ' -f 1
}


# Main script
echo "Calling calculate_sum..."
# Capture the stdout of the function into the 'result' variable
result=$(calculate_sum 15 30)
echo "The sum is: $result"

echo ""
echo "Calling get_first_word..."
my_sentence="This is a sentence."
first=$(get_first_word "$my_sentence") # Capture the first word
echo "Original: '$my_sentence'"
echo "First word: '$first'"

# --- Pitfall: Handling other output ---
# If a function prints diagnostic messages AND the result, capture will get
both!
noisy_function() {
  echo "Debug: Starting calculation..." >&2 # Send debug to stderr
  local result=100
  echo "Debug: Finished calculation." >&2 # Send debug to stderr
  echo "$result" # Send actual result to stdout
}

echo ""
echo "Calling noisy_function..."
noise_result=$(noisy_function)
echo "Result from noisy function: '$noise_result'"
```

Run it:

```
$ ./function_return_data.sh
Calling calculate_sum...
The sum is: 45

Calling get_first_word...
Original: 'This is a sentence.'
First word: 'This'

Calling noisy_function...
Debug: Starting calculation...
Debug: Finished calculation.
Result from noisy function: '100'
```

Key points for returning data via stdout:

- The function should ideally *only* print the exact data you want to capture to standard output.
- Any other diagnostic or progress messages should be printed to **standard error (stderr)** using redirection (>&2), as shown in noisy_function. This keeps stdout clean for the calling command substitution.
- Command substitution $(...) captures only stdout.
- This method is primarily suited for returning a single piece of string data. Returning multiple distinct values or complex data structures usually requires more advanced techniques or different scripting languages.

Choose the return method based on what the function needs to communicate: exit status for success/failure, standard output for data results.

Variable Scope Revisited

We saw earlier that variables defined in a script are local to that script's process unless exported. What about variables defined *inside* a function? By default, variables defined inside a function are **global** within the script! This means they are visible and can be modified by code outside the function after the function has been called. This can lead to unexpected side effects and bugs, especially in larger scripts.

Example (Problematic):

```
#!/bin/bash
# scope_problem.sh
```

```
my_func() {
    # 'counter' is implicitly global here!
    counter=10
    echo "[Inside function] Counter is: $counter"
}

# Global variable
counter=1
echo "[Before call] Counter is: $counter"

my_func # Call the function

echo "[After call] Counter is: $counter" # Ouch! The function changed our global
variable!
```

Run it:

```
$ ./scope_problem.sh
[Before call] Counter is: 1
[Inside function] Counter is: 10
[After call] Counter is: 10
```

The counter variable defined inside my_func overwrote the global counter defined outside. This is generally bad practice.

To prevent this and make variables truly local to the function where they are defined, use the local keyword when declaring them *inside* the function.

Example (Corrected using local):

```
#!/bin/bash
# scope_fixed.sh

my_func() {
    # Declare 'counter' as local to this function
    local counter=10
    local temp_var="Function specific" # Also local
    echo "[Inside function] Local Counter is: $counter"
    echo "[Inside function] Temp var is: $temp_var"
}

# Global variable
counter=1
echo "[Before call] Global Counter is: $counter"
```

```
my_func # Call the function

echo "[After call] Global Counter is: $counter" # Unchanged!
echo "[After call] Trying to access temp_var: $temp_var" # Doesn't exist here
```

Run it:

```
$ ./scope_fixed.sh
[Before call] Global Counter is: 1
[Inside function] Local Counter is: 10
[Inside function] Temp var is: Function specific
[After call] Global Counter is: 1
[After call] Trying to access temp_var:
```

Rule: Always use the `local` **keyword** to declare variables inside your functions unless you have a very specific reason to modify a global variable intentionally (which should be rare and carefully considered). This practice greatly improves the robustness and predictability of your scripts by preventing functions from accidentally interfering with each other or the main script logic through shared global variables.

Including Code from Other Files

As you write more scripts and develop useful functions (like logging, error handling, common tasks), you might want to reuse these functions across *multiple* different scripts without copying and pasting the function definitions everywhere.

The `source` command (which has a shortcut: a single dot `.`) executes commands from a specified file *in the current shell environment*. This is different from running a script directly (`./script.sh`), which usually runs in a subshell. When you `source` a file containing function definitions, those functions become defined and available in your *current* script.

Steps:

1. **Create a "library" file:** Create a separate file (e.g., `my_lib.sh`) containing only function definitions (and perhaps common variable exports).

   ```
   # my_lib.sh - A library of useful functions

   # Function to log messages with a timestamp
   log_message() {
   ```

```
    local timestamp=$(date +"%Y-%m-%d %H:%M:%S")
    # Print to stderr so it doesn't interfere with stdout capture
    echo "[$timestamp] $1" >&2
}

# Function to add two numbers (returns via stdout)
add_numbers() {
    local sum=$(($1 + $2))
    echo "$sum"
}
```

2. **Source the library file in your main script:** Use source or . followed by the path to the library file.

```bash
#!/bin/bash
# main_script.sh - Uses functions from my_lib.sh

# Source the library file (assuming it's in the same directory)
# Use '.' or 'source'
. ./my_lib.sh
# Alternatively: source ./my_lib.sh

# Now we can use the functions defined in my_lib.sh
log_message "Starting the main script."

num1=50
num2=75

log_message "Calculating sum of $num1 and $num2..."
total=$(add_numbers $num1 $num2) # Capture result from function

log_message "Calculation complete."
echo "The total is: $total"

log_message "Main script finished."
```

Make both files executable (optional for the library, needed for the main script) and run main_script.sh:

```
$ chmod +x main_script.sh
$ ./main_script.sh
[2024-07-23 22:45:10] Starting the main script.
[2024-07-23 22:45:10] Calculating sum of 50 and 75...
[2024-07-23 22:45:10] Calculation complete.
The total is: 125
```

```
[2024-07-23 22:45:10] Main script finished.
```

Using `source` to create function libraries is a powerful technique for organizing larger scripting projects and promoting code reuse.

Chapter Summary

In this chapter, you learned how to structure your shell scripts more effectively using **functions**. We explored the benefits: **modularity**, **reusability**, **readability**, and **maintainability**. You learned the syntax for defining (`my_func() { ... }`) and calling functions. We saw how functions receive **arguments** (`$1`, `$@`, etc.) similar to scripts, but specific to the function call. You learned the two primary ways functions "return" information: via **exit status** using `return N` (for success/failure signaling) and via **standard output** combined with command substitution `result=$(...)` (for returning data). Crucially, you understood the importance of variable scope and why you should **always use** `local` to declare variables inside functions. Finally, we saw how the `source` (or `.`) command allows you to load function definitions from external library files, enabling better code organization and reuse across multiple scripts.

Functions are essential building blocks for writing non-trivial shell scripts. They allow you to abstract complexity and build more robust, understandable automation tools. As your scripts become more complex, however, finding and fixing errors becomes more challenging. In the next chapter, we'll tackle the essential skill of **debugging** your shell scripts, exploring techniques and tools to help you track down and resolve problems effectively.

15

Debugging Scripts and Handling Errors

As you start writing more sophisticated scripts using functions (Chapter 14), loops (Chapter 13), and conditionals (Chapter 12), you'll inevitably encounter something every programmer faces: bugs. Little gremlins seem to creep into the code, causing scripts to behave unexpectedly, produce strange output, or simply crash. Don't worry – this is a completely normal part of the process! Learning how to find and fix these errors, known as **debugging**, is just as important as learning how to write the script in the first place. Furthermore, writing robust scripts involves anticipating potential problems and handling them gracefully, rather than just letting the script fail abruptly. This chapter equips you with essential techniques for debugging your Bash scripts and strategies for handling errors effectively, making your automation tools more reliable and easier to troubleshoot.

Finding Bugs

Before diving into debugging tools, let's look at some common pitfalls that often lead to bugs in shell scripts:

1. **Quoting Errors:** Forgetting to quote variables ("$my_var") or using the wrong type of quotes (single '...' vs. double "...") is perhaps the most frequent

source of errors, especially when variables contain spaces, newlines, or special characters. This can lead to commands receiving incorrect arguments or failing entirely. Revisit Chapter 11 if you're unsure about quoting rules.

2. **Spaces Around = in Assignments:** Remember `my_var="value"` is correct, while `my_var = "value"` is wrong and will likely result in a "command not found" error.

3. **Forgetting Spaces in [or [[:** The test command `[` and the compound command `[[` need spaces immediately after the opening bracket(s) and before the closing bracket(s) (e.g., `[[ "$a" == "$b" ]]`). Missing these spaces leads to syntax errors.

4. **Confusing String and Integer Comparisons:** Using string operators (`=`, `!=`) for numbers or integer operators (`-eq`, `-ne`) for non-integer strings will produce incorrect results or errors.

5. **Path Issues:** Assuming a command or file is in the current directory or `$PATH` when it isn't. Always use appropriate paths (`./script.sh`, `/usr/local/bin/mytool`, `$HOME/data/file.txt`).

6. **Permissions:** Forgetting to make a script executable (`chmod +x`) or trying to read/write files or directories without the necessary permissions (Chapter 5).

7. **Off-by-One Errors:** In loops, especially C-style `for` loops or `while` loops with counters, incorrectly setting the start/end condition or increment step.

8. **Command Substitution Issues:** Forgetting the `$(...)` syntax or having commands inside the substitution fail silently or produce unexpected output.

9. **Scope Mistakes:** Accidentally modifying global variables inside functions because the `local` keyword was omitted (Chapter 14).

Being aware of these common mistakes can help you spot potential problems even before you run your script.

Debugging Techniques

When your script doesn't work as expected, how do you figure out *why*? Here are several techniques, ranging from simple to more powerful.

Printing Variables

This is the simplest and often the first debugging technique people use – sometimes affectionately called "caveman debugging." Simply insert `echo` statements at various points in your script to print the values of variables or simple status messages. This helps you track the script's flow and see if variables contain the values you expect them to.

```bash
#!/bin/bash
# buggy_script.sh - Needs debugging

source_dir="/path/to/source" # Might be incorrect path
dest_file="backup.tar.gz"

# --- Add echo for debugging ---
echo "Debug: Source directory is set to: $source_dir"
echo "Debug: Destination file is set to: $dest_file"
# ----------------------------

# Check if source exists
if [[ ! -d "$source_dir" ]]; then
    # --- Add echo for debugging ---
    echo "Debug: Source directory check failed!"
    # ----------------------------
    echo "Error: Source directory '$source_dir' not found." >&2
    exit 1
fi

echo "Attempting to create archive..."
# The 'tar' command might fail if source_dir is wrong
tar czf "$dest_file" "$source_dir"

# --- Add echo for debugging ---
echo "Debug: tar command exit status: $?"
# ----------------------------

echo "Archive creation finished."
```

By adding these echo "Debug: ..." lines, you can run the script and see the actual values being used and where the logic might be going wrong (e.g., discovering $source_dir wasn't what you thought, or seeing the non-zero exit status from tar). Once you've fixed the bug, remember to remove or comment out your debug echo statements.

Tracing Execution

While echo is useful for specific points, sometimes you need a broader view of exactly *what* commands the shell is executing and *how* variables and wildcards are being expanded. Bash provides **execution tracing** for this, enabled by the set -x option.

When `set -x` is active, Bash prints each command to standard error *before* it executes it, showing the command *after* all expansions (variables, command substitution, wildcards) have taken place. This gives you a detailed trace of the script's actions.

You can enable it for the whole script by adding `set -x` near the top, or enable it just for a specific section and then disable it with `set +x`.

```bash
#!/bin/bash
# trace_demo.sh

filename_pattern="*.txt"
output_file="summary.log"

echo "Starting script..."

# Enable tracing for the critical section
set -x

# Count the matching files
count=$(ls $filename_pattern | wc -l)

# Did ls or wc -l work? What did $count become?
echo "Found $count files matching '$filename_pattern'." > "$output_file"

# Disable tracing
set +x

echo "Script finished. Check $output_file."
```

Let's run this (assuming `planets.txt`, `data.txt` etc. exist):

```
$ ./trace_demo.sh
Starting script...
# Tracing output starts here (lines usually prefixed with '+')
+ ls --color=auto celestial_bodies.txt data.txt file_a.txt mydata.txt
planets.txt planets_backup.txt planets_desc.txt planets_inner.txt planets_v1.txt
playground_contents.txt # ls command after wildcard expansion
+ wc -l # wc command receives output from ls via pipe
+ count=10 # Assignment after command substitution completes
+ echo 'Found 10 files matching '\''*.txt'\''.' # echo command after
variable/quote expansion
# Tracing output ends here
Script finished. Check summary.log.
```

The lines starting with + (the prefix character can vary, often set by the PS4 variable) show the exact commands executed after the shell performed all its substitutions. You can see the wildcard *.txt expanded, the result assigned to count, and the final echo command with the variable $count replaced by 10. This is incredibly useful for diagnosing issues related to variable expansion, wildcard matching, or command substitution.

Exiting on Error

By default, if a command within your script fails (returns a non-zero exit status), the script simply continues executing the subsequent commands. This can lead to strange behavior or errors later on if subsequent commands depended on the failed one succeeding.

The set -e option tells Bash to **exit immediately** if any simple command exits with a non-zero status. This can make scripts safer by preventing them from continuing after an unexpected failure.

```
#!/bin/bash
# set_e_demo.sh

# Enable exit on error
set -e

echo "Step 1: Creating directory..."
mkdir /definitely/not/writable # This command will likely fail

echo "Step 2: This message will probably NOT be printed."
ls

echo "Script finished? (Only if mkdir succeeded)"
```

Run it:

```
$ ./set_e_demo.sh
Step 1: Creating directory...
mkdir: cannot create directory '/definitely': Permission denied
# Script exits here due to 'set -e' and the mkdir failure.
# The 'Step 2' echo and ls commands are never reached.
```

Pros: Helps catch errors early and prevents cascading failures. **Cons:**

- Can make debugging harder if the script exits before you can examine state.

- Might exit unexpectedly if a command sometimes fails non-critically.
- Doesn't apply to commands whose exit status is part of a conditional test (if, while, until, &&, ||). You still need explicit error checking in those cases.

Use set -e cautiously, understanding its implications. You can disable it with set +e.

Treating Unset Variables as Errors

Typo-ing a variable name is a common mistake (echo "$user_nmae" instead of echo "$user_name"). By default, Bash treats an unset variable as empty, which might hide the typo and lead to unexpected behavior.

The set -u option tells Bash to treat referencing an unset variable (other than special parameters like $* or $@) as an error, causing the script to exit immediately.

```
#!/bin/bash
# set_u_demo.sh

# Enable exit on unset variables
set -u

correct_var="Hello"
echo "Correct variable: $correct_var"

echo "Now trying to access a typo..."
echo "Typo variable: $coorect_var" # Misspelled variable name

echo "This message will NOT be printed."
```

Run it:

```
$ ./set_u_demo.sh
Correct variable: Hello
Now trying to access a typo...
./set_u_demo.sh: line 10: coorect_var: unbound variable
# Script exits here due to 'set -u' and the unset variable access.
```

Using set -u is highly recommended during development as it helps catch typos in variable names very effectively. You can disable it with set +u.

Combining Options: You can combine these set options: set -eux enables exit-on-error, unset-variable-error, and command tracing simultaneously, which is a powerful combination for debugging.

Understanding Exit Statuses

We've mentioned exit statuses frequently. Let's formalize their role in debugging and error handling. Every command that finishes execution returns an integer **exit status** code.

- **Exit Status 0:** Conventionally indicates **success**.
- **Exit Status 1-255:** Conventionally indicates **failure**. Different non-zero values *can* be used to signify different types of errors, although many commands simply return 1 for any general failure.

The shell automatically stores the exit status of the *most recently executed foreground command* in the special variable $?. You can check this immediately after a command runs.

```
$ ls /etc/passwd # Command succeeds
/etc/passwd
$ echo $?
0

$ ls /etc/no_such_file # Command fails
ls: cannot access '/etc/no_such_file': No such file or directory
$ echo $?
2 # 'ls' uses specific non-zero codes for different errors

$ grep "root" /etc/passwd > /dev/null # Found pattern, grep succeeds
$ echo $?
0

$ grep "nosuchuser" /etc/passwd > /dev/null # Pattern not found, grep fails
$ echo $?
1

$ true # Command that always succeeds
$ echo $?
0

$ false # Command that always fails
$ echo $?
1
```

Checking $? is fundamental for determining if a critical command in your script succeeded or failed.

Checking Command Success in Scripts

How do you use $? effectively within a script?

Method 1: Direct Check with if (Most Common)

The if statement naturally checks the exit status of the command provided as its condition. This is the cleanest and most common way to check command success.

```
if cp source.txt destination.txt
then
  echo "File copied successfully."
else
  echo "Error: File copy failed! Exit status: $?" >&2
  # Optionally exit the script if the copy was critical
  # exit 1
fi
```

Here, the else block executes only if the cp command returns a non-zero exit status.

Method 2: Explicit Check of $?

You can run the command and then immediately check the value of $?.

```
tar czf backup.tar.gz /my/data
tar_exit_status=$? # Store immediately! $? changes after every command.

if [[ "$tar_exit_status" -ne 0 ]]; then
  echo "Error: tar command failed with status $tar_exit_status" >&2
  exit 1
fi

echo "Backup completed successfully."
```

This is slightly more verbose but necessary if you need the specific exit code for detailed error reporting or if you need to run other commands between the critical command and the check (which would overwrite $?). Remember to capture $? into another variable *immediately* if you need to preserve it.

Handling Errors Gracefully

Simply letting a script exit on error (set -e) or checking $? isn't always enough. A robust script should ideally:

1. **Detect** critical errors.
2. **Report** the error clearly to the user (usually on `stderr`).
3. Perform any necessary **cleanup** (e.g., remove temporary files).
4. **Exit** with an appropriate non-zero status code to signal failure to any calling process or script.

We can combine conditionals and functions to create reusable error handlers.

```bash
#!/bin/bash
# graceful_error_handling.sh

# Function to print error messages to stderr and exit
error_exit() {
  local message="$1"
  local exit_code="${2:-1}" # Default exit code is 1 if not provided

  echo "ERROR: $message" >&2
  exit "$exit_code"
}

# --- Main Script ---
TEMP_DIR="/tmp/myscript_temp_$$" # $$ is the current script's PID

echo "Creating temporary directory: $TEMP_DIR"
mkdir "$TEMP_DIR"
if [[ "$?" -ne 0 ]]; then
  error_exit "Could not create temporary directory '$TEMP_DIR'." 5
fi

echo "Attempting to copy critical config..."
cp /etc/important.conf "$TEMP_DIR/"
if [[ "$?" -ne 0 ]]; then
  # Cleanup before exiting
  echo "Performing cleanup..." >&2
  rm -rf "$TEMP_DIR"
  error_exit "Failed to copy important config file." 6
fi

echo "Processing data (simulation)..."
sleep 2
# Imagine a failure here
if false; then # Replace 'false' with a real command that might fail
  # Cleanup before exiting
  echo "Performing cleanup..." >&2
  rm -rf "$TEMP_DIR"
  error_exit "Data processing step failed!" 7
fi
```

```
echo "Cleaning up temporary directory..."
rm -rf "$TEMP_DIR"
if [[ "$?" -ne 0 ]]; then
    # Can't use error_exit here as it exits, maybe just warn
    echo "Warning: Failed to remove temporary directory '$TEMP_DIR'." >&2
fi

echo "Script completed successfully."
exit 0
```

This script defines an `error_exit` function for consistent error reporting and exiting. It checks the status of critical commands (`mkdir`, `cp`) and calls `error_exit` upon failure, ensuring cleanup actions (`rm -rf`) are attempted before exiting.

Trapping Signals (`trap`) for Cleanup

What if the user interrupts your script with `Ctrl+C` (`SIGINT`), or the system tries to shut it down (`SIGTERM`) before it finishes normally? If your script created temporary files or acquired locks, these might be left behind, causing problems later.

The `trap` command allows your script to detect and intercept (**trap**) specific signals, executing a predefined list of commands before actually exiting. This is invaluable for ensuring proper cleanup happens, regardless of how the script terminates.

Basic Syntax:

```
trap 'commands_to_run' SIGNAL1 [SIGNAL2 ...]
```

- `'commands_to_run'`: A string containing the command(s) to execute when one of the specified signals is received.
- `SIGNAL1 [SIGNAL2 ...]`: The signal names (e.g., `INT`, `TERM`, `HUP`) or numbers (e.g., `2, 15, 1`) to trap.

A very common and useful signal name is `EXIT`. This is a pseudo-signal provided by Bash that triggers the trap command *whenever the script exits for any reason* – whether normally, via an `exit` command, or due to a signal.

Example with Cleanup:

```
#!/bin/bash
```

```
# trap_demo.sh

TEMP_FILE="/tmp/my_temp_data.$$" # Unique temp file using PID

# --- Cleanup Function ---
# It's good practice to put cleanup actions in a function
cleanup() {
  echo "" # Newline after potential Ctrl+C
  echo "Cleaning up temporary file: $TEMP_FILE"
  # Use 'rm -f' to avoid errors if the file doesn't exist
  rm -f "$TEMP_FILE"
}

# --- Trap Setup ---
# Execute the 'cleanup' function when the script exits (normally or via signal)
# or receives INT (Ctrl+C) or TERM signals.
trap cleanup EXIT INT TERM

# --- Main Script ---
echo "Creating temporary file: $TEMP_FILE"
date > "$TEMP_FILE"
if [[ "$?" -ne 0 ]]; then
  echo "ERROR: Failed to create temp file." >&2
  exit 1 # Trap will still run the cleanup function on exit
fi

echo "Script running... PID: $$"
echo "Temporary data:"
cat "$TEMP_FILE"
echo ""
echo "Press Ctrl+C or wait 15 seconds to exit..."

sleep 15

echo "Script finished normally."
# Cleanup function will be called automatically by the EXIT trap here.
```

How to Test:

1. Run ./trap_demo.sh. Let it finish normally after 15 seconds. Observe the "Cleaning up..." message appear at the very end.
2. Run ./trap_demo.sh again. This time, press Ctrl+C while it's sleeping. Observe that the "Cleaning up..." message *still* appears before the script fully exits.

The `trap cleanup EXIT INT TERM` line ensures that the `cleanup` function is executed reliably, preventing temporary files from being left behind. This makes your scripts much tidier and less likely to cause issues due to leftover artifacts.

Chapter Summary

In this chapter, you learned that debugging is an essential skill for any scripter. We identified common mistakes like quoting errors and path issues. You were equipped with practical **debugging techniques**, including simple variable printing with `echo`, detailed command tracing using `set -x`, making scripts fail early on errors with `set -e`, and catching typos with `set -u`. We reinforced the importance of checking command **exit statuses** (`$?`) and demonstrated how to do this cleanly using `if` or explicit checks. You learned strategies for **handling errors gracefully** by detecting failures, reporting them clearly (to `stderr`), performing cleanup, and exiting with non-zero status codes, potentially using helper functions. Finally, you discovered the powerful `trap` command, especially `trap cleanup EXIT`, for ensuring critical **cleanup actions** run reliably even if the script is interrupted or exits unexpectedly.

By applying these debugging and error-handling techniques, you can write scripts that are not only functional but also robust, reliable, and easier to maintain. Now that you can manage script flow and handle errors, we need to tackle more complex text manipulation. While `grep`, `sed`, and `awk` (Chapter 9) are powerful, sometimes you need even more precise pattern matching capabilities, especially for validating input or extracting specific data from complex strings. In the next chapter, we will dive deep into the fascinating world of **Regular Expressions (Regex)**.

16

Regular Expressions (Regex)

You've built an impressive toolkit: navigating, managing files, handling permissions, controlling processes, writing functions, making decisions, and looping through tasks. You've also encountered powerful text processing tools like `grep`, `sed`, and `awk` back in Chapter 9. We briefly mentioned that these tools can use "patterns," but we didn't delve deeply into *what* those patterns really are. Now, it's time to unlock one of the most potent text-manipulation concepts available on the command line: **Regular Expressions**, often shortened to **regex** or **regexp**. Think of regex as super-powered search patterns, far more flexible and precise than the simple wildcards (`*`, `?`) you learned for filenames. Mastering regex will dramatically enhance your ability to search text, validate data, extract specific information, and perform complex substitutions, elevating your command-line and scripting skills to a new level.

What Are Regular Expressions?

At its core, a regular expression is a **sequence of characters that defines a search pattern**. This pattern isn't usually meant to match literally; instead, it uses special characters, called **metacharacters**, alongside literal characters to describe *what* kind of text sequence you're looking for.

Imagine you need to find not just the literal word "color" but also its British spelling "colour". Or perhaps you need to find any line that starts with a date in the format YYYY-MM-DD, or validate whether user input looks like a valid email address. Simple string matching or filename wildcards aren't precise enough for these tasks. Regular expressions provide the grammar needed to describe these complex patterns.

Why are they so important in Linux? Because so much in Linux revolves around text:

- Configuration files (`/etc/`)
- Log files (`/var/log/`)
- Command output
- Scripting languages
- Data files (CSV, custom formats)

Regex allows you to interact with all this text data in incredibly sophisticated ways directly from the command line or within your scripts, using tools like `grep`, `sed`, `awk`, and many others (including programming languages like Python, Perl, JavaScript, etc.).

Think of simple string searching as looking for an exact house address. Think of filename wildcards (`*.txt`) as looking for all houses on a specific street ending in ".txt". Regular expressions are like giving the search detailed architectural plans – "find all two-story houses built between 1980 and 1990 with a red door and exactly three windows on the front." They offer vastly more descriptive power.

Basic vs. Extended Regular Expressions

As regular expressions evolved within the Unix world, different tools adopted slightly different syntaxes or "flavors" of regex. The two main flavors you'll encounter in traditional command-line tools are:

1. **Basic Regular Expressions (BRE):** This is the older style. In BRE, most characters are treated literally, and only a few metacharacters (`.` `*` `[ ]` `^` `$`) have special meaning by default. Other metacharacters, like those for grouping `()` or specifying quantities `{}`, *must* be preceded by a backslash (`\`) to give them their special meaning (e.g., `\( \) \{ \}`). Tools like standard `grep` and standard `sed` use BRE by default.

2. **Extended Regular Expressions (ERE):** This is a more modern style where more metacharacters (`?`, `+`, `(`, `)`, `{`, `}`, `|`) have special meaning by default,

requiring *fewer* backslashes. This generally makes ERE patterns cleaner and easier to read. Tools like egrep (or grep -E), awk, and sed -E (or sed -r on some systems) use ERE.

Which should you learn? While it's good to be aware of BRE because you'll encounter it, **we will primarily focus on ERE syntax** in this chapter. It's generally less cumbersome and more consistent with regex usage in modern programming languages. Just remember that if you're using standard grep or sed without the -E option, you might need to add backslashes before characters like (,), {, }, ?, +, or | for them to work as metacharacters.

Key Metacharacters (ERE Focus)

Let's dive into the building blocks of regular expressions. These special characters and sequences allow you to define your patterns. We'll use the ERE syntax primarily.

Anchors

Anchors don't match characters themselves, but rather *positions* within the line.

- ^ (Caret): Matches the **beginning** of the line.
  - ^Error: Matches lines that *start* with the word "Error".
- $ (Dollar): Matches the **end** of the line.
  - done$: Matches lines that *end* with the word "done".
  - ^OnlyThis$: Matches lines containing *only* the exact text "OnlyThis" and nothing else.

Character Classes

These match specific types or sets of characters.

- . (Dot/Period): Matches **any single character** except, usually, a newline character.
  - c.t: Matches "cat", "cot", "c@t", "c5t", etc., but not "ct" or "colt".
- [...] (Square Brackets): Matches **any one character** listed inside the brackets. This defines a **character set**.
  - [aeiou]: Matches any single lowercase vowel.
  - [Tt]: Matches an uppercase 'T' or a lowercase 't'.
  - **Ranges:** You can specify ranges using a hyphen.

- [a-z]: Matches any single lowercase letter.
- [A-Z]: Matches any single uppercase letter.
- [0-9]: Matches any single digit.
- [a-zA-Z0-9]: Matches any single alphanumeric character.

- **Negated Sets:** If the first character inside the brackets is a caret ^, it matches any single character *not* in the set.
  - [^0-9]: Matches any single character that is *not* a digit.
  - [^aeiou]: Matches any single character that is *not* a lowercase vowel.

- **POSIX Character Classes:** These are special notations written inside [[]] within the main [...]. They are often more portable than explicit ranges, especially across different language settings (locales).

  - [[:alnum:]]: Alphanumeric characters ([a-zA-Z0-9]).
  - [[:alpha:]]: Alphabetic characters ([a-zA-Z]).
  - [[:digit:]]: Digits ([0-9]). Equivalent to \d in some regex flavors.
  - [[:lower:]]: Lowercase letters ([a-z]).
  - [[:upper:]]: Uppercase letters ([A-Z]).
  - [[:space:]]: Whitespace characters (space, tab, newline, etc.). Equivalent to \s in some regex flavors.
  - [[:punct:]]: Punctuation characters.
  - [[:xdigit:]]: Hexadecimal digits ([0-9a-fA-F]).
  - Example: [[:digit:]]{3} matches exactly three digits. [^[:alpha:]] matches any non-alphabetic character.

Quantifiers

Quantifiers specify how many times the *immediately preceding* character, character set, or group must occur to match.

- * (Asterisk): Matches the preceding element **zero or more** times.
  - ab*c: Matches "ac", "abc", "abbc", "abbbc", etc.
  - .*: Matches *any* sequence of characters (zero or more), often used as a "match anything" wildcard within a line.
- + (Plus): Matches the preceding element **one or more** times.
  - ab+c: Matches "abc", "abbc", "abbbc", etc., but *not* "ac".
- ? (Question Mark): Matches the preceding element **zero or one** time (makes it optional).
  - colou?r: Matches "color" or "colour".
- {n}: Matches the preceding element exactly n times.

- [0-9]{5}: Matches exactly five digits (like a US ZIP code).
- {n,}: Matches the preceding element n or more times.
  - a{3,}: Matches "aaa", "aaaa", "aaaaa", etc.
- {n,m}: Matches the preceding element at least n times, but no more than m times.
  - x{2,4}: Matches "xx", "xxx", or "xxxx".

Greediness: By default, *, +, and ? are **greedy**. They try to match the longest possible string that satisfies the pattern. For example, given the text <h1>Title</h1>, the regex <.+> would match the entire string <h1>Title</h1>, not just <h1>. Making quantifiers "lazy" or "non-greedy" (to match the shortest possible string) often involves adding a ? after the quantifier (e.g., *?, +?), but support for this varies across tools and regex engines. For basic usage, assume greediness.

Alternation

- | (Pipe/Vertical Bar): Acts like an **OR**. Matches the expression on its left *or* the expression on its right.
  - cat|dog: Matches lines containing "cat" or "dog".
  - ^(Error|Warning): Matches lines starting with either "Error" or "Warning". Use parentheses () to limit the scope of the alternation if needed.

Grouping and Capturing

- (...) (Parentheses):
  1. **Groups** parts of the expression together, allowing you to apply a quantifier to the entire group.
     - (ab)+: Matches "ab", "abab", "ababab", etc.
     - ^(Warning|Error):: Matches lines starting with "Warning:" or "Error:".
  2. **Captures** the text matched by the part of the pattern inside the parentheses. This captured text can be reused later, particularly in substitutions (sed) or by programming languages. These are called **capturing groups**. (Non-capturing groups (?:...) exist but are more advanced).

Escaping Metacharacters

What if you want to match a character that normally has a special meaning? For example, how do you match a literal dot (.) or a literal asterisk (*)? You **escape** it with a backslash (\).

- \.: Matches a literal dot/period.
- *: Matches a literal asterisk.
- \?: Matches a literal question mark.
- \\: Matches a literal backslash.
- \$: Matches a literal dollar sign (usually needed only if it's not at the end).
- \^: Matches a literal caret (usually needed only if it's not at the beginning).
- \[and \]: Matches literal square brackets.
- \(and \): Matches literal parentheses (needed in ERE if you don't want grouping).

Using Regex with `grep`

`grep` is the primary tool for *finding* lines matching a regex.

- `grep 'REGEX' file...` **(BRE)**: Remember to escape (,), {, } etc. if you need their special meaning. Often simpler patterns work fine.
- `grep -E 'REGEX' file...` or `egrep 'REGEX' file...` **(ERE)**: Recommended for complex patterns involving +, ?, |, (), {}.

Examples (using `grep -E`):

Let's create a sample log file `app.log`:

```
2024-07-24 10:00:15 INFO: Application startup successful.
2024-07-24 10:01:02 WARN: Disk space low on /dev/sda1 (95% used).
2024-07-24 10:01:30 INFO: User 'alice' logged in from 192.168.1.100.
2024-07-24 10:02:05 ERROR: Database connection failed: timeout expired.
2024-07-24 10:03:00 INFO: User 'bob' updated profile.
2024-07-24 10:03:15 WARN: Configuration reload requested.
```

- **Find lines starting with a date (YYYY-MM-DD):**

  ```
  $ grep -E '^[0-9]{4}-[0-9]{2}-[0-9]{2}' app.log
  # All lines should match
  ```

- **Find only ERROR or WARN messages:**

```
$ grep -E '^(ERROR|WARN):' app.log # Doesn't match sample data! Why?
(Anchored to start)
# No output or error

$ # Correction: The date/time comes first! Match anywhere on line for
now:
$ grep -E '(ERROR|WARN):' app.log
2024-07-24 10:01:02 WARN: Disk space low on /dev/sda1 (95% used).
2024-07-24 10:02:05 ERROR: Database connection failed: timeout expired.
2024-07-24 10:03:15 WARN: Configuration reload requested.

$ # More precise: Match date, time, then ERROR or WARN
$ grep -E '^[0-9]{4}(-[0-9]{2}){2} [0-9]{2}(:[0-9]{2}){2} (ERROR|WARN):'
app.log
2024-07-24 10:01:02 WARN: Disk space low on /dev/sda1 (95% used).
2024-07-24 10:02:05 ERROR: Database connection failed: timeout expired.
2024-07-24 10:03:15 WARN: Configuration reload requested.
```

- **Find login messages containing an IP address (simplified regex):**

```
# Very basic IP regex: 3 digits, dot, repeat 4 times
$ grep -E '[0-9]{1,3}\.[0-9]{1,3}\.[0-9]{1,3}\.[0-9]{1,3}' app.log
2024-07-24 10:01:30 INFO: User 'alice' logged in from 192.168.1.100.
```

(Note: Real IP address validation regex is much more complex!)

- **Extract only the IP addresses (-o option):**

```
$ grep -o -E '[0-9]{1,3}\.[0-9]{1,3}\.[0-9]{1,3}\.[0-9]{1,3}' app.log
192.168.1.100
```

Using Regex with sed

sed uses regex primarily in the address part (to select lines) and in the s (substitute)
command's FIND_PATTERN.

- sed '/REGEX/command' file... **(BRE):** Selects lines matching the BRE
  REGEX for the command (e.g., d for delete).
- sed 's/BRE_REGEX/REPLACEMENT/FLAGS' file... **(BRE):** Performs substitution using BRE. Remember \(\) for capturing.
- sed -E ... **(ERE):** Use -E to enable extended regex in addresses and the s
  command. Capturing uses (...).

Substitution with Backreferences:

This is where capturing groups (...) become powerful. In the `REPLACEMENT` string of the s command, `\1` refers to the text captured by the *first* (...) group in the regex, `\2` refers to the second, and so on.

Examples (using `sed -E`):

- **Swap username and IP address in login messages:**

```
$ grep -E "logged in" app.log | sed -E "s/User '([^']*)' logged in from
(.*)\./User '\1' logged in from IP: \2/"
2024-07-24 10:01:30 INFO: User 'alice' logged in from IP: 192.168.1.100
```

  - `'([^']*)'`: Captures the username (any character except ') into group `\1`.
  - `(.*)`: Captures the rest of the string (the IP address) into group `\2`.
  - `User '\1' ... IP: \2`: Reconstructs the string using the captured groups.
- **Add quotes around the percentage in the WARN message:**

```
$ grep WARN app.log | sed -E 's/([0-9]+%) used/"\1" used/'
2024-07-24 10:01:02 WARN: Disk space low on /dev/sda1 ("95%") used.
```

  - `([0-9]+%)`: Captures one or more digits followed by % into group `\1`.
  - `"\1"`: Replaces the match with the captured group enclosed in quotes.

Using Regex with awk

awk inherently uses ERE for its pattern matching, making it very natural to use regex.

- **Line Selection:** `/REGEX/ { action }` - Executes the action only for lines matching the ERE REGEX.

```
$ awk '/WARN|ERROR:/ { print $0 }' app.log
2024-07-24 10:01:02 WARN: Disk space low on /dev/sda1 (95% used).
2024-07-24 10:02:05 ERROR: Database connection failed: timeout expired.
2024-07-24 10:03:15 WARN: Configuration reload requested.
```

- **Field Matching (~ Operator):** Check if a specific field matches a regex.

```
# Print the message ($4 onwards) for lines where field 3 is WARN or
ERROR
$ awk '$3 ~ /^(WARN|ERROR):$/ { $1=$2=$3=""; print substr($0,4) }'
app.log
 Disk space low on /dev/sda1 (95% used).
 Database connection failed: timeout expired.
 Configuration reload requested.
```

- **Built-in Functions:** awk has functions like gsub(/REGEX/, "replacement", target_string) for global substitution within strings inside the action block, offering more flexibility than sed sometimes.

Practical Regex Examples

Let's solidify with a few more common scenarios.

- **Validating a Simple North American Phone Number (e.g., NNN-NNN-NNNN):**

```
phone="123-456-7890"
if [[ "$phone" =~ ^[0-9]{3}-[0-9]{3}-[0-9]{4}$ ]]; then
  echo "'$phone' looks like a valid format."
else
  echo "'$phone' does NOT match the format."
fi
```

(Note the =~ operator used within [[...]] for ERE matching in Bash itself).

- **Extracting URLs (Simplified):**

```
# Assuming URLs start with http:// or https://
grep -o -E 'https?://[^[:space:]"]+' some_web_page.html
```

- **Filtering Apache Log for POST Requests:**

```
# Apache combined log format often has method in quotes
grep -E ' \"POST ' access.log
```

Pitfalls and Tips

- **Complexity Kills:** Regex can become extremely complex and difficult to read (sometimes called "line noise"). Strive for clarity. Add comments in your scripts explaining non-obvious regex patterns. Sometimes, multiple simpler steps are better than one monstrous regex.
- **Performance:** Very complex regex patterns, especially those involving extensive backtracking, can be slow on large inputs. Consider the efficiency implications.
- **Greediness:** Remember quantifiers like * and + are greedy. .* will match as much as possible. Be mindful of this when trying to match specific segments.
- **Quoting:** Always enclose your regex pattern in single ('...') or double ("...") quotes when passing it as an argument to commands like grep or sed. This prevents the shell from trying to interpret metacharacters like * or | before the command sees them. Single quotes are often safer unless you *need* variable expansion within the regex.
- **Test, Test, Test:** Use tools like grep -E or online regex testers (like regex101.com) to experiment with your patterns on sample data before embedding them in critical scripts. Test edge cases!

Chapter Summary

Regular expressions are a fundamental and powerful tool for text manipulation on the Linux command line and in scripting. You learned the difference between **BRE** and **ERE**, focusing on the cleaner **ERE** syntax. We explored key **metacharacters**, including **anchors** (^, $), various **character classes** (., [...], [[:class:]]), **quantifiers** (*, +, ?, {}), **alternation** (|), **grouping/capturing** (()), and the necessity of **escaping** (\). You saw practical examples of using regex with grep -E (for finding lines and extracting matches with -o), sed -E (especially for substitution using **backreferences** like \1), and awk (for selecting lines and matching fields with ~). Remember to test your patterns and prioritize clarity.

Mastering regex takes practice, but the payoff in text-processing power is immense. Now that you can craft intricate patterns and write well-structured, error-handled scripts with functions, loops, and conditionals, it's time to consider best practices that make your scripts not just functional, but truly professional. In the next chapter, we'll discuss style, formatting, security considerations, and portability to help you write better, more maintainable shell scripts.

17

Writing Better Scripts

You've journeyed from executing single commands to crafting intricate shell scripts complete with variables, logic, loops, functions, error handling, and even powerful regular expressions (Chapter 16). Your scripts can *do* things now, automating tasks and acting as custom tools. That's fantastic! But there's a difference between a script that merely *works* and a script that is well-crafted – one that is readable, reliable, secure, easy to debug, and simple for others (or your future self!) to understand and modify. This chapter focuses on elevating your scripting game by exploring best practices, style guidelines, security considerations, and maintainability techniques. Think of it as learning scripting hygiene – the habits that distinguish professional, dependable scripts from quick-and-dirty hacks.

Readability Counts

A script might function perfectly, but if it looks like a jumbled mess, it's going to be a nightmare to maintain or debug later. Consistent formatting and a clean style make your code vastly easier to read and understand at a glance.

Indentation

Indentation is key to visually representing the structure of your code, especially with control flow statements like `if`, `for`, `while`, `case`, and function definitions. Code blocks associated with these structures should be indented consistently.

- **Choose a Style:** Decide whether to use spaces (commonly 2 or 4) or tabs for indentation. Neither is inherently "better," but **consistency is paramount**. Pick one style and stick to it throughout your script (and ideally, across your projects). Mixing tabs and spaces can lead to visual inconsistencies in different editors.
- **Apply it Consistently:** Indent the code between `then` and `fi`/`else`/`elif`, between `do` and `done`, between `case` patterns and `;;`, and within function braces `{ ... }`.

Good:

```
if [[ "$debug_mode" -eq 1 ]]; then
  echo "Debug mode enabled."
  set -x # Indented command
fi

for file in *.log; do
  if [[ -f "$file" ]]; then
    echo "Processing $file..." # Further indentation
    # More commands...
  fi
done
```

Bad (Harder to Read):

```
if [[ "$debug_mode" -eq 1 ]]; then
echo "Debug mode enabled."
set -x
fi

for file in *.log; do
if [[ -f "$file" ]]; then
echo "Processing $file..."
# More commands...
fi
done
```

Spacing

Appropriate use of whitespace (spaces and blank lines) significantly improves readability.

- **Around Operators:** Place spaces around comparison operators within `[[` ... `]]` (e.g., `[[ "$a" == "$b" ]]` is easier to read than `[["$a"=="$b"]]`) and around arithmetic operators in `$((...))` (e.g., `$((count + 1))` vs `$((count+1))`).
- **After Keywords:** Put a space after keywords like `if`, `while`, `for`, `case`, `function`.
- **Before Braces:** Often, a space before an opening curly brace `{` in function definitions or command groups improves clarity.
- **Blank Lines:** Use blank lines (sparingly) to separate logical blocks of code, such as between function definitions or before major sections of logic within a script. This breaks up dense code and signals logical separation.

Line Length

Extremely long lines of code are hard to read and often require horizontal scrolling. Aim for a reasonable maximum line length, traditionally around 80 characters, though slightly longer (e.g., 100-120) is often acceptable on modern displays.

If a command or expression is naturally long, you can use a backslash (\) at the end of a line to continue the command on the next line. Use this sparingly, as it can sometimes make code harder to follow than simply breaking the task into multiple commands or using intermediate variables.

Example of Line Continuation:

```
# Long 'find' command broken up for readability
find /data/archive -type f \
  -name "*.gz" \
  -mtime +30 \
  -print0 | \
  xargs -0 --no-run-if-empty rm -f
```

Consistency

Above all, be **consistent** with your chosen style for indentation, spacing, naming, and formatting throughout your script and related projects. A consistent style makes the code predictable and easier for anyone (including yourself) to scan and understand quickly.

Meaningful Variable and Function Names

Choosing good names for your variables and functions is one of the simplest yet most effective ways to make your scripts understandable. Cryptic names force anyone reading the code to constantly decipher their meaning.

- **Be Descriptive:** Names should clearly indicate the purpose or content of the variable or function. `input_filename` is vastly better than `ifn` or `x`. `calculate_disk_usage` is clearer than `cdu` or `do_it`.
- **Avoid Ambiguity:** Choose names that aren't easily confused with other variables, functions, or standard commands.
- **Follow Conventions:** While Bash doesn't enforce strict rules, common conventions improve consistency:
  - **Local Variables/Functions:** `lowercase_with_underscores` (snake_case) is very common and readable (e.g., `log_file`, `process_input`).
  - **Environment Variables/Constants:** `UPPERCASE_WITH_UNDERSCORES` (SCREAMING_SNAKE_CASE) is the standard convention for environment variables (`PATH`, `HOME`) and often used for constants defined within a script (e.g., `readonly MAX_RETRIES=5`).
- **Length:** Prefer clarity over extreme brevity, but avoid excessively long names if a shorter, clear alternative exists.

Think about someone reading your code for the first time. Will the names make sense without needing extra explanation?

Effective Commenting Strategies

Comments (`# ...`) explain your code to human readers; the shell ignores them. Good comments are essential for maintainability.

- **Explain the *Why*, Not Just the *What*:** Don't just restate the obvious command. Comments should explain the *purpose* or *intent* behind a piece of code, especially if the logic is complex, non-intuitive, or involves a workaround.
  - **Bad:** `# Increment counter` followed by `((counter++))`
  - **Good:** `# Counter tracks number of files processed successfully` followed by `((counter++))`
- **Header Block:** Start your scripts with a comment block containing metadata:
  - Script purpose/description.
  - Usage instructions (arguments, options).

- Author (optional).
- Date created/modified (optional).
- Dependencies (optional).
- **Function Comments:** Precede each function definition with comments explaining:
  - What the function does.
  - What arguments ($1, $2, etc.) it expects.
  - What it "returns" (exit status or data via stdout).
- **Inline Comments:** Use comments alongside specific lines only when necessary to clarify a particular step or variable. Don't over-comment simple code.
- **Keep Comments Updated:** This is critical! An outdated comment that describes code that has changed is misleading and worse than no comment at all. When you modify code, update the relevant comments.
- **Use Blank Lines and Comment Blocks:** Structure comments logically, using blank lines or comment blocks (# --- Section Name ---) to separate sections.

When *Not* to Use a Shell Script

Shell scripting is incredibly powerful for automating command sequences, managing files, and gluing other programs together. However, it has limitations. Knowing when *not* to use a shell script is as important as knowing how to write one. Shell scripts might be the wrong tool when your task involves:

1. **Complex Data Structures:** Bash arrays are fairly basic (mostly indexed lists of strings). If you need complex structures like nested arrays, dictionaries/hashes/maps, trees, or objects, languages like Python, Perl, or Ruby offer much better built-in support.
2. **Extensive Mathematical Operations:** Bash arithmetic is limited to integers. For floating-point math, complex calculations, or statistical analysis, dedicated tools (bc, awk) or languages like Python (with libraries like NumPy/SciPy) are far more suitable.
3. **Complex String Manipulation/Parsing:** While sed, awk, and regex are powerful, parsing structured formats like JSON, XML, or complex binary data is often much easier and safer using dedicated libraries available in other languages.
4. **Building Graphical User Interfaces (GUIs):** Shell scripting is fundamentally text-based.

5. **Large, Complex Applications:** For projects requiring intricate logic, many modules, object-oriented design, or extensive libraries, a general-purpose programming language is usually a better fit.
6. **Performance-Critical Tasks:** While shell scripts can be fast for I/O-bound tasks (running external commands), computationally intensive algorithms will generally run much slower than equivalent code written in a compiled language (like C, Go) or even faster interpreted languages like Python.

Don't try to force a shell script to do something it's not well-suited for. **Choose the right tool for the job.** Often, a simple shell script is perfect, but sometimes switching to Python or another language will save you significant time and effort in the long run.

Portability Concerns

Throughout this book, we've focused on **Bash**, the Bourne Again SHell, because it's the most common interactive shell on Linux. However, the baseline standard for shells on UNIX-like systems is defined by **POSIX** (Portable Operating System Interface). The standard command interpreter specified by POSIX is typically referred to as /bin/sh. On many systems, /bin/sh might be Bash running in POSIX mode, or it could be a different, simpler shell like dash (common on Debian/Ubuntu) or ksh.

Why does this matter? If you write a script using features specific to Bash (**Bashisms**) and try to run it using /bin/sh (e.g., by using the shebang #!/bin/sh or running sh your_script.sh), it might fail or behave incorrectly on systems where /bin/sh isn't Bash.

Common Bashisms to be aware of:

- [[...]]: The double-bracket conditional compound command. POSIX standard is [...] (the test command).
- ((...)): Arithmetic evaluation. POSIX standard is $((...)) or the external expr command.
- function **keyword:** Optional in Bash, but the POSIX standard is just function_name() { ... }.
- **Arrays (Advanced):** While POSIX defines basic indexed arrays accessed like ${array[0]}, many advanced array features and associative arrays are Bash-specific.
- **Process Substitution:** <(...) and >(...).
- **Here Strings:** <<< "string".
- **Regular Expression Matching:** The =~ operator inside [[...]].

- **Certain Options:** Some options to built-in commands like `echo -e` (interpret escapes) or `read -p` (prompt) are not guaranteed by POSIX.

When to care about portability:

- **System Scripts:** Writing scripts intended to run during system boot or as part of core system utilities (e.g., init scripts, systemd unit file scripts) often requires sticking strictly to POSIX `sh` features for maximum compatibility.
- **Cross-Platform Scripts:** If your script needs to run reliably on various UNIX-like systems (Linux distributions, macOS, BSD variants) where `/bin/sh` might not be Bash.
- **Collaborative Projects:** If project guidelines require POSIX compliance.

What to do:

- **Be Aware:** Recognize which features are Bash-specific.
- **Use `#!/bin/bash`:** If your script relies on Bashisms, explicitly use the `#!/bin/bash` shebang to ensure it's run with Bash. Accept the dependency on Bash being available.
- **Stick to POSIX:** If portability is paramount, consciously limit yourself to features defined by the POSIX standard for `sh`.
- **Use `shellcheck`:** This is an excellent static analysis tool that can examine your script and warn you about syntax errors, semantic problems, non-portable constructs (potential Bashisms if targeting `sh`), and common pitfalls. Install it (`sudo apt install shellcheck`, `sudo dnf install ShellCheck`) and run it regularly on your scripts: `shellcheck your_script.sh`.

Security Considerations in Shell Scripting

When scripts handle user input, process files, or especially when they run with elevated privileges (`sudo`), security becomes critical. Careless scripting can open up vulnerabilities.

- **Always Quote Variables:** We can't stress this enough. Unquoted variables containing filenames or user input are vulnerable to **word splitting** and **globbing** (wildcard expansion). A filename like `"file with spaces.txt"` used unquoted (`rm $filename`) becomes `rm file with spaces.txt`, potentially deleting unrelated files. Always use double quotes: `rm "$filename"`. Use `"$@"` to handle arguments safely.

- **Avoid Command Injection:** This happens when user-supplied input is treated as part of a command to be executed. Never construct command strings by directly embedding raw user input.

  - **Dangerous:** `USER_INPUT="; rm -rf /"; COMMAND="echo $USER_INPUT"; eval "$COMMAND"`
  - **Safer:** Pass user input as distinct *arguments* to commands. `USER_PATTERN="..."; FILENAME="..."; grep "$USER_PATTERN" "$FILENAME"` (Here, `grep` treats `$USER_PATTERN` as data, not commands).
  - **Avoid** `eval`: The `eval` command executes its arguments as a shell command. It's powerful but extremely dangerous if used with untrusted input. Avoid it unless absolutely necessary and you have rigorously validated the input first.

- **Secure Temporary Files:** Don't use predictable filenames in shared directories like `/tmp` (e.g., `/tmp/myscript.pid`). Another process could potentially interfere with or read/write to that file. Use the `mktemp` command to securely create temporary files or directories with unique, unpredictable names. Use `trap` (Chapter 15) to ensure these temporary files are cleaned up.

```
TEMP_FILE=$(mktemp) || exit 1
trap 'rm -f "$TEMP_FILE"' EXIT
echo "Data" > "$TEMP_FILE"
# ... use $TEMP_FILE ...
```

- **Permissions:**

  - Give your scripts the minimum necessary permissions. Don't make scripts world-writable unless required.
  - Avoid running scripts as `root` unless absolutely necessary. If only specific commands within the script need root privileges, consider running just those commands via `sudo` inside the script (and configure `/etc/sudoers` carefully to allow only those specific commands if possible).

- **Environment:** Be cautious if your script runs with elevated privileges (e.g., via `sudo` or `su`). A user might manipulate environment variables like `PATH` or `IFS` before running the script to influence its behavior. Consider setting a known-safe `PATH` at the beginning of privileged scripts: `export PATH="/bin:/sbin:/usr/bin:/usr/sbin"`.

Keeping Scripts Maintainable

Maintainability means making scripts easy to understand, modify, and debug over time.

- **Use Functions:** Break logic into reusable functions (Chapter 14).
- **Define Constants:** Store fixed values (paths, URLs, default settings) in variables (often uppercase and maybe `readonly`) near the top of the script. This makes them easy to find and change if needed.

```
readonly LOG_DIR="/var/log/myapp"
readonly MAX_ATTEMPTS=3
```

- **Robust Error Handling:** Check return codes (`$?`), use `set -e`/`set -u` appropriately, provide clear error messages to `stderr`, use `trap` for cleanup (Chapter 15).
- **Meaningful Exit Codes:** Use `exit 0` for success and specific non-zero codes (`exit 1`, `exit 2`, etc.) to indicate different failure modes. This allows other scripts or monitoring systems to determine *why* your script failed.
- **Validate Input:** Check user input and command-line arguments early in the script to ensure they are valid before proceeding. Fail fast if input is incorrect.
- **Keep it Simple (KISS):** Avoid overly complex shell gymnastics or obscure syntax if a straightforward approach achieves the same result. Clarity often trumps minor efficiency gains in scripting.
- **Version Control:** Use a version control system like `git` (briefly mentioned in Chapter 19) to track changes to your scripts, collaborate, and revert mistakes.

Chapter Summary

Writing functional scripts is just the beginning; writing *good* scripts requires discipline and attention to best practices. In this chapter, we emphasized the importance of **readability** through consistent formatting, indentation, spacing, and meaningful naming conventions. We stressed effective **commenting** to explain the *why*, not just the *what*. You learned to recognize when shell scripting might not be the best tool and considered **portability** issues related to Bashisms vs. POSIX sh, highlighting the usefulness of `shellcheck`. We covered critical **security considerations**, focusing on proper quoting, avoiding command injection, using `mktemp`, and handling permissions carefully. Finally, we discussed strategies for **maintainability**, including using functions, constants, robust error handling, meaningful exit codes, input validation, and keeping things simple.

By adopting these practices, you'll write scripts that are not only powerful automation tools but also professional, reliable, secure, and easy for yourself and others to work with long-term. With these well-crafted scripts in hand, you're perfectly positioned to have the system run them for you automatically. In the next chapter, we'll explore cron, the standard Linux utility for scheduling your scripts and commands to run at specific times or intervals.

18

Automating the Future

You've built a solid foundation. You can navigate, manage files, understand permissions, control processes, write functions, handle errors (Chapter 15), and even employ sophisticated text processing techniques (Chapter 16). You've learned how to write scripts (Chapter 10) that automate sequences of tasks, following the best practices we discussed in Chapter 17. But automation truly comes alive when you don't even have to *manually run* your scripts. What if you could schedule your backup script to run every night automatically? Or have a cleanup script execute every weekend? Or perhaps run a system check every hour? Linux provides a standard, reliable mechanism for exactly this kind of time-based task scheduling: the **cron** system. This chapter introduces you to cron, showing you how to define scheduled jobs and have the system execute your commands and scripts automatically, turning your automation efforts into truly hands-off operations.

Introducing cron

At the heart of scheduled tasks on most Linux and UNIX-like systems lies the cron **daemon**. A daemon is simply a program that runs continuously in the background, waiting to perform actions. The cron daemon wakes up every minute, checks its configuration files for any jobs scheduled to run at that specific minute, and executes them if found.

Think of cron as a meticulous, tireless personal assistant for your computer. You give it a list of instructions (your commands or scripts) and a precise schedule for each instruction. The assistant then consults its schedule every minute and carries out the tasks exactly when you specified, without you needing to remind it.

cron is incredibly reliable and has been the standard scheduler for decades. It's perfect for automating routine maintenance, data processing, reporting, and any other task that needs to happen on a regular basis.

The Crontab File

How do you give cron its list of scheduled tasks? You define them in special configuration files called **crontabs** (short for "cron tables"). There are two main types:

1. **System-wide Crontabs:** Located primarily in /etc/crontab and the /etc/cron.d/ directory. These are usually managed by the system administrator (root) and are used for system-level tasks (like log rotation, system updates checks, etc.). The format often includes an extra field specifying *which user* the command should run as.
2. **Per-user Crontabs:** Each user on the system can have their own personal crontab file, typically stored in a system directory like /var/spool/cron/crontabs/ but managed via a dedicated command (crontab). Commands listed in a user's crontab run *as that user*. This is the type we will focus on, as it's what you'll use for scheduling your own scripts and tasks.

Structure and Syntax

The core of using cron lies in understanding the format of a crontab entry. Each line in a crontab file that isn't a comment (#) or an environment setting defines a single scheduled job. A job definition consists of six fields, separated by spaces or tabs, followed by the command to execute:

```
# Minute Hour DayOfMonth Month DayOfWeek Command
#  ┌─────── minute (0 - 59)
#  │ ┌───── hour (0 - 23)
#  │ │ ┌─── day of month (1 - 31)
#  │ │ │ ┌─ month (1 - 12) OR jan,feb,mar,...
#  │ │ │ │ ┌ day of week (0 - 6) (Sunday=0 or 7) OR sun,mon,tue,...
#  │ │ │ │ │
# * * * * * command to execute
```

Let's break down each time field:

Field	Description	Allowed Values	Special Characters
Minute	Minute of hour	`0 - 59`	`*, */n, n-m, a,b,c`
Hour	Hour of day	`0 - 23` (24-hour format)	`*, */n, n-m, a,b,c`
DayOfMonth	Day of month	`1 - 31`	`*, */n, n-m, a,b,c, L, W?`
Month	Month of year	`1 - 12` OR `jan, feb, ... dec`	`*, */n, n-m, a,b,c`
DayOfWeek	Day of week	`0 - 7` (0 or 7 is Sunday) OR `sun, mon, ... sat`	`*, */n, n-m, a,b,c, #, L?`
Command	The command or script path to execute	Any valid shell command	N/A

(Note: Special characters like `L` and `W` might be available in some `cron` implementations but are less standard).

Special Characters:

- `*` (Asterisk): Represents "any" value or "every". An asterisk in the Minute field means "every minute". An asterisk in the Hour field means "every hour".
- `,` (Comma): Separates multiple specific values. `1,15,30` in the Minute field means "at minute 1, 15, AND 30".
- `-` (Hyphen): Specifies a range of values. `9-17` in the Hour field means "every hour from 9 AM through 5 PM (inclusive)".
- `*/n` (Slash): Specifies step values. `*/15` in the Minute field means "every 15 minutes" (i.e., at 0, 15, 30, 45). `*/2` in the Hour field means "every 2 hours".

Important Note on DayOfMonth vs. DayOfWeek: If *both* DayOfMonth and DayOfWeek are specified (i.e., not `*`), the command will run if *either* condition matches. For example, `0 0 1 * 1` would run at midnight on the 1st of every month *AND* also every Monday. If you want it to run only when it's *both* the 1st and a Monday, you need to handle that logic *within* your script or use system-specific `cron` features if available. Usually, you set one of these fields to `*` if you are specifying the other.

Examples:

- `0 5 * * * /home/jane/bin/daily_backup.sh`
  - Runs `/home/jane/bin/daily_backup.sh` every day at 5:00 AM. (Minute 0, Hour 5, any DayOfMonth, any Month, any DayOfWeek).

- `*/15 * * * * /usr/local/bin/check_status`
  - Runs `/usr/local/bin/check_status` every 15 minutes, every hour, every day. (Every 15th minute, any Hour, ...).
- `0 0 1,15 * * /home/jane/bin/monthly_report.sh`
  - Runs `/home/jane/bin/monthly_report.sh` at midnight (00:00) on the 1st and 15th of every month.
- `30 18 * * 1-5 /home/jane/scripts/end_of_workday.sh`
  - Runs `/home/jane/scripts/end_of_workday.sh` at 6:30 PM (18:30) every Monday through Friday. (Minute 30, Hour 18, any DayOfMonth, any Month, DayOfWeek 1 through 5).
- `@reboot /home/jane/scripts/run_on_startup.sh`
  - Special string `@reboot`: Runs the command once shortly after the system boots up. Other special strings like `@hourly`, `@daily`, `@weekly`, `@monthly`, `@yearly` are often supported as shortcuts for common schedules (e.g., `@daily` is usually equivalent to `0 0 * * *`).

Editing Your Crontab

You should **never** directly edit the crontab files in `/var/spool/cron/crontabs/`. Instead, always use the `crontab` command, which provides locking and basic syntax checking.

The command to edit your personal crontab is:

```
$ crontab -e
```

- This command will open your user crontab file in the default text editor specified by your system or your `VISUAL` or `EDITOR` environment variables (often `nano` or `vim`).
- If this is the first time you're running it, it might create a new, empty file for you, possibly containing some comments explaining the format.
- Add your job definition lines, one per line, following the six-field syntax.
- Save the file and exit the editor.
- Upon exiting, the `crontab` command will check the syntax of your changes. If it finds errors, it will usually prompt you to re-edit the file. If the syntax is okay, it will install the new crontab, and you'll typically see a message like `crontab: installing new crontab`.

Example: Let's add a job to append the current date and time to a log file every minute.

1. Run `crontab -e`.

2. Add the following line to the file (using an absolute path for `date` just to be safe, though it's usually in the default cron path):

```
# Log the time every minute
* * * * * /bin/date >> /home/jane/playground/cron_log.txt
```

3. Save and exit the editor.

Now, wait a minute or two, and check the contents of the log file:

```
$ tail ~/playground/cron_log.txt
Tue Jul 23 23:15:01 EDT 2024
Tue Jul 23 23:16:01 EDT 2024
Tue Jul 23 23:17:01 EDT 2024
```

It worked! `cron` is executing the `/bin/date` command every minute and appending its output.

Listing and Removing Cron Jobs

- `crontab -l` **(List):** To view the currently installed crontab for your user without opening the editor, use:

```
$ crontab -l
# Log the time every minute
* * * * * /bin/date >> /home/jane/playground/cron_log.txt
```

- `crontab -r` **(Remove):** To **completely remove** your entire crontab file, use:

```
$ crontab -r
```

Warning: This command offers **no confirmation** by default! It immediately deletes your entire crontab. It's generally much safer to use `crontab -e` and manually delete the specific lines you no longer want, then save the file. Use `crontab -r` with extreme caution.

Understanding the Cron Environment

This is one of the most common sources of problems when scheduling jobs with cron. Commands that run perfectly when you type them in your interactive shell might fail mysteriously when run via cron. This is usually because cron **executes commands in a very minimal, restricted environment**.

Compared to your interactive shell session:

- **Minimal PATH:** The $PATH environment variable is typically much shorter, often containing only basic system directories like /usr/bin:/bin. It likely won't include directories like /usr/local/bin, /snap/bin, or custom directories in your home directory (~/bin, ~/scripts) unless explicitly set.
- **No Shell Startup Files:** cron does *not* typically run your .bashrc, .bash_profile, or .profile. This means any aliases, functions, environment variables (EDITOR, custom PATH extensions), or shell options defined there will *not* be available to your cron jobs.
- **Different Working Directory:** Commands executed via cron usually run with your **home directory** as the current working directory, regardless of where you were when you edited the crontab. If your script relies on being in a specific directory to find relative files, it will fail.
- **No Interactive Terminal:** There's no connected terminal (tty), so commands expecting interactive input will hang or fail.

Solutions:

1. **Use Absolute Paths:** The most reliable solution is to use the full, absolute path for *every* command and script you call within your crontab's command field. Instead of my_backup_script.sh, use /home/jane/scripts/my_backup_script.sh. Instead of date, use /bin/date (you can find paths using which command_name, e.g., which date).

2. **Set PATH in the Crontab:** You can define environment variables directly within the crontab file itself. These definitions apply to all subsequent commands in that crontab. Setting a PATH near the top is common practice:

   ```
   PATH=/usr/local/bin:/usr/bin:/bin:/home/jane/bin

   # Now you might be able to use commands without full paths if they're in
   the specified PATH
   0 5 * * * daily_backup.sh
   ```

```
*/15 * * * * check_status
```

This is convenient but still requires knowing which directories your commands live in.

3. `cd` **in the Command:** If your script needs to run from a specific directory, include the `cd` command *as part of the cron command string*, using && to chain it with the actual command.

```
0 1 * * * cd /path/to/my/project && ./run_data_processing.sh
```

This ensures the script runs in the correct working directory.

4. **Source Environment Files (Use Cautiously):** You *can* sometimes source your profile within the cron command (e.g., `. ~/.profile && command`), but this can be fragile and pull in more environment than needed. It's usually better to explicitly set required variables or use absolute paths.

Recommendation: Using **absolute paths** for commands and scripts in your crontab entries is generally the most robust and least surprising approach.

Redirecting Output from Cron Jobs

By default, any output (`stdout or stderr`) produced by a command run via `cron` is collected and emailed to the owner of the crontab (usually you). If your jobs run frequently or produce lots of output, this can quickly fill up your mailbox.

It's often better to redirect the output to log files, just like you learned in Chapter 6.

- **Redirect** `stdout` **to a file (overwrite):**

```
0 0 * * * /path/to/script.sh > /home/jane/logs/script.log
```

- **Redirect** `stdout` **(append):**

```
0 0 * * * /path/to/script.sh >> /home/jane/logs/script.log
```

- **Redirect** `stderr` **to a separate file (append):**

```
0 0 * * * /path/to/script.sh >> /home/jane/logs/script.log 2>>
/home/jane/logs/script.error.log
```

- **Redirect both `stdout` and `stderr` to the same file (append):** (Using the traditional, portable syntax)

```
0 0 * * * /path/to/script.sh >> /home/jane/logs/script.log 2>&1
```

Or using Bash/Zsh shorthand if your `cron` uses such a shell (check your system's `/etc/crontab` `SHELL` variable):

```
# May not work on all systems
# 0 0 * * * /path/to/script.sh &>> /home/jane/logs/script.log
```

- **Discard all output (if you're *sure* you don't need it):**

```
0 0 * * * /path/to/script.sh > /dev/null 2>&1
```

`/dev/null` is a special system file that acts like a black hole – anything sent there disappears. Redirecting here suppresses all output and prevents emails. Use this only for commands you are certain produce no useful output or errors, or after thorough testing. Logging errors is usually preferable.

Properly managing output redirection is key to keeping your system clean and diagnosing issues when jobs don't run as expected.

Common Automation Examples

What kinds of tasks are typically automated with `cron`?

- **Backups:** Running your custom backup script (`rsync`, `tar`, etc.) nightly or weekly.

```
30 2 * * 0 /home/jane/bin/full_backup.sh >> /home/jane/logs/backup.log
2>&1
```

- **System Updates Check (Non-interactive):** Checking for updates daily (specific command depends on distribution).

```
# Example for Debian/Ubuntu
0 4 * * * /usr/bin/apt update > /dev/null && /usr/bin/apt list --
upgradable > /home/jane/logs/updates_available.txt
```

- **Log File Rotation/Cleanup:** Running scripts to archive or delete old log files.

```
0 0 * * 0 /home/jane/scripts/cleanup_old_logs.sh
```

- **Running Monitoring Scripts:** Checking disk space, website availability, or application health periodically.

```
*/10 * * * * /home/jane/scripts/check_website.sh || echo "Website check
failed at $(date)" >> /home/jane/logs/monitor_errors.log
```

- **Fetching Data:** Downloading reports or data feeds at regular intervals.

```
0 6 * * * /usr/bin/curl -o /home/jane/data/daily_report.csv
https://example.com/reports/today
```

Debugging Cron Jobs

When a cron job doesn't work:

1. **Check Cron Daemon Logs:** Look in system logs like /var/log/syslog, /var/log/messages, or /var/log/cron (location varies by distribution). Search for entries related to CRON or the specific command that should have run. These logs might show basic execution info or errors from the cron daemon itself.
2. **Check Mail:** If you haven't redirected output, check the local mail for your user (often using the mail command). Error messages might have been sent there.
3. **Redirect Output:** Modify the crontab entry to redirect *both* stdout and stderr to a log file (>> /path/to/job.log 2>&1). Run the job (or wait for it) and then examine the log file for any error messages produced by your command or script.
4. **Verify Paths:** Double-check that you are using absolute paths for all commands and scripts in the crontab entry. Use which command_name to confirm paths.

5. **Verify Permissions**: Ensure the user whose crontab it is has permission to execute the script and any commands within it, and permission to read/write any files it accesses.

6. **Test Command Manually (Simulating Cron Env)**: Try running the *exact* command string from the crontab entry directly in your terminal, but simulate the cron environment:
    - Use `cd $HOME` first to match the likely working directory.
    - Use `env -i PATH=/usr/bin:/bin bash -c 'your_full_cron_command_string'` to run the command with a minimal environment similar to cron's. This can often reveal path or environment-related issues.

Debugging cron jobs often boils down to understanding the restricted environment they run in and ensuring paths, permissions, and output redirection are handled correctly.

Chapter Summary

This chapter introduced you to `cron`, the standard Linux mechanism for scheduling commands and scripts to run automatically at specified times or intervals. You learned about the `cron` daemon and the structure of **crontab** files, mastering the six-field syntax (`*, */n, n-m, a,b,c`) used to define job schedules. We covered the standard commands for managing your user crontab: `crontab -e` (edit), `crontab -l` (list), and the cautious `crontab -r` (remove). Critically, you learned about the minimal **cron environment** and why using **absolute paths** or setting `PATH` explicitly is crucial for reliability. We also explored how to **redirect output** (`stdout` and `stderr`) from cron jobs to prevent unwanted emails and facilitate logging. Finally, we looked at common automation examples and strategies for debugging cron jobs when they misbehave.

You can now take the scripts you write and have your system execute them automatically, freeing you from repetitive manual execution. This brings us near the end of our core journey. In the final chapter, we'll look beyond the basics, touching upon a few more essential command-line tools (like `tar` and `ssh`), introducing the vital concept of version control with `git`, and suggesting avenues for further learning in the vast world of Linux.

## 19

Beyond the Basics

What an incredible journey we've had! Starting with your first tentative steps into the terminal in Chapter 1, you've learned to navigate the Linux filesystem, manage files and permissions, harness the power of pipes and redirection, tame processes, customize your shell environment (Chapter 8), write conditional logic and loops, organize code with functions, debug effectively (Chapter 15), wield regular expressions (Chapter 16), follow best practices (Chapter 17), and even automate tasks with `cron` (Chapter 18). You've built a formidable foundation in Linux command-line operations and shell scripting.

While we've covered the essential core, the Linux world is vast and filled with specialized tools. This final chapter aims to briefly introduce a few more indispensable utilities you'll likely encounter, give you a crucial pointer towards version control with `git`, and offer some suggestions for where your Linux adventure might take you next. Consider this a launching pad for your continued exploration.

Working with Archives

As you work with files, especially when sharing projects, making backups, or downloading software source code, you'll frequently encounter **archives**. An archive is a single file that contains multiple other files and directories, preserving their structure and permissions. Often, archives are also **compressed** to reduce their size.

tar

The classic Linux/UNIX utility for creating and manipulating archives is `tar` (originally **t**ape **ar**chiver, though now mostly used with disk files). `tar` itself doesn't compress; it just bundles files together. It's almost always used in combination with a compression utility like `gzip` or `bzip2`.

Common `tar` Operations:

You control `tar` using options, often strung together without leading hyphens. The most crucial option is `-f`, which specifies the archive filename; it should almost always be the *last* option in the group.

- **Create (c) an archive:**

    - `-c`: Create a new archive.
    - `-v`: Verbosely list files being processed.
    - `-f filename`: Use the specified archive `filename`.
    - `-z`: Filter the archive through `gzip` (creates `.tar.gz` or `.tgz`).
    - `-j`: Filter the archive through `bzip2` (creates `.tar.bz2`).

    Example: Creating a gzipped archive:

    ```
    $ # Archive the 'Notes' and 'TextFiles' directories into archive.tar.gz
    $ tar -czvf my_playground_backup.tar.gz Notes/ TextFiles/
    Notes/
    Notes/2024-07-23/
    Notes/2024-07-23/draft_notes.txt
    Notes/important_notes.txt
    TextFiles/
    TextFiles/report_feb.log
    TextFiles/report_jan.log
    TextFiles/summary.txt
    TextFiles/project_plan.doc
    TextFiles/report.log
    $ ls -lh my_playground_backup.tar.gz
    -rw-r--r-- 1 jane jane 1.5K Jul 24 10:15 my_playground_backup.tar.gz
    ```

- **List (t) archive contents:**

    - `-t`: List the contents without extracting.

    ```
    $ tar -tvf my_playground_backup.tar.gz
    drwxr-xr-x jane/jane         0 2024-07-23 20:15 Notes/
    drwxr-xr-x jane/jane         0 2024-07-23 21:20 Notes/2024-07-23/
    ```

```
-rw-r--r-- jane/jane          0 2024-07-23 21:20
Notes/2024-07-23/draft_notes.txt
-rw-r--r-- jane/jane          0 2024-07-23 15:30
Notes/important_notes.txt
drwxr-xr-x jane/science_proj 0 2024-07-23 14:45 TextFiles/
-rw-r--r-- jane/science_proj 0 2024-07-23 14:45 TextFiles/report_feb.log
# ... output continues ...
```

- **Extract (x) from an archive:**

  - -x: Extract files from the archive.
  - tar automatically detects gzip/bzip2 compression during extraction based on the file extension, so you often don't need -z or -j explicitly when extracting (though including them doesn't hurt).

```
$ mkdir restore_location
$ cd restore_location
$ tar -xvf ../my_playground_backup.tar.gz # Extract here
Notes/
Notes/2024-07-23/
Notes/2024-07-23/draft_notes.txt
# ... output continues ...
$ ls
Notes  TextFiles
```

tar is fundamental for packaging files on Linux. You'll constantly encounter .tar.gz or .tar.bz2 files.

Other Tools

- gzip/gunzip: Compresses/decompresses single files (usually used with tar). Creates/uses .gz files. zcat displays contents of a .gz file without decompressing.
- bzip2/bunzip2: Another compression tool, often providing better compression than gzip but potentially slower. Creates/uses .bz2 files. bzcat displays contents.
- zip/unzip: Creates/extracts .zip archives, which combine archiving and compression. While less common natively on Linux than tar, zip is widely used for compatibility with Windows systems.

Basic Networking Commands

Networking is a huge topic, but here are a few essential command-line tools for basic network diagnostics and interaction.

ping

`ping` sends a small data packet (ICMP ECHO_REQUEST) to a target host to see if it responds. It's the fundamental tool for checking if a machine is reachable over the network and measuring basic round-trip time (latency).

```
$ ping google.com
PING google.com (142.250.191.142) 56(84) bytes of data.
64 bytes from ord38s30-in-f14.1e100.net (142.250.191.142): icmp_seq=1 ttl=115
time=12.5 ms
64 bytes from ord38s30-in-f14.1e100.net (142.250.191.142): icmp_seq=2 ttl=115
time=12.8 ms
64 bytes from ord38s30-in-f14.1e100.net (142.250.191.142): icmp_seq=3 ttl=115
time=12.2 ms
^C # Press Ctrl+C to stop
--- google.com ping statistics ---
3 packets transmitted, 3 received, 0% packet loss, time 2003ms
rtt min/avg/max/mdev = 12.238/12.515/12.810/0.235 ms
```

No response usually indicates a network problem (or the host blocking pings).

ip addr

This command shows details about your system's network interfaces (Ethernet cards, Wi-Fi adapters, loopback). It replaces the older `ifconfig` command on most modern Linux systems.

```
$ ip addr show
1: lo: <LOOPBACK,UP,LOWER_UP> mtu 65536 qdisc noqueue state UNKNOWN group
default qlen 1000
    link/loopback 00:00:00:00:00:00 brd 00:00:00:00:00:00
    inet 127.0.0.1/8 scope host lo
       valid_lft forever preferred_lft forever
    inet6 ::1/128 scope host
       valid_lft forever preferred_lft forever
2: eth0: <BROADCAST,MULTICAST,UP,LOWER_UP> mtu 1500 qdisc fq_codel state UP
group default qlen 1000
    link/ether 00:11:22:aa:bb:cc brd ff:ff:ff:ff:ff:ff
```

```
    inet 192.168.1.150/24 brd 192.168.1.255 scope global dynamic eth0
       valid_lft 85833sec preferred_lft 85833sec
    inet6 fe80::211:22ff:feaa:bbcc/64 scope link
       valid_lft forever preferred_lft forever
# ... other interfaces like wlan0 ...
```

Look for `inet` lines to see IPv4 addresses and `inet6` for IPv6 addresses associated with interfaces like `eth0` (Ethernet) or `wlan0` (Wireless).

hostname

Simply shows the configured name of your Linux system.

```
$ hostname
my-linux-box
```

ssh

Secure **SH**ell (`ssh`) is the standard, encrypted way to log into and execute commands on remote Linux/UNIX machines.

Basic Syntax:

```
ssh username@remote_host_address
```

Replace `username` with your username on the remote machine and `remote_host_address` with its IP address or hostname. The first time you connect, it will ask you to verify the host's key. Then, it will typically prompt for your password on the remote machine.

```
$ ssh jane@server.example.com
The authenticity of host 'server.example.com (10.0.5.20)' can't be established.
ED25519 key fingerprint is SHA256:xxxxxxxxxxxxxxxxxxxxxxxxxxxxxxxxxxxxxxxxxxxx.
Are you sure you want to continue connecting (yes/no/[fingerprint])? yes
Warning: Permanently added 'server.example.com' (ED25519) to the list of known
hosts.
jane@server.example.com's password:
Last login: Wed Jul 24 09:30:00 2024 from client.local
[jane@server ~]$ # You are now logged into the remote server!
[jane@server ~]$ exit # Log out from the remote server
logout
Connection to server.example.com closed.
```

```
$ # You are back on your local machine
```

Passwordless Login: For frequent access or automation, setting up **SSH key-based authentication** (using `ssh-keygen` and `ssh-copy-id`) is highly recommended. It's more secure and convenient than using passwords.

scp

Built on `ssh`, scp allows you to securely copy files between machines.

Syntax:

- **Local to Remote:** `scp /path/to/local/file username@remote_host:/path/to/remote/destination`
- **Remote to Local:** `scp username@remote_host:/path/to/remote/file /path/to/local/destination`

Example:

```
$ # Copy my_script.sh from local machine to jane's home dir on server
$ scp ./my_script.sh jane@server.example.com:~/scripts/
jane@server.example.com's password:
my_script.sh                        100%  512    15.3KB/s   00:00

$ # Copy remote log file from server to local current directory (.)
$ scp jane@server.example.com:/var/log/app.log .
jane@server.example.com's password:
app.log                             100% 2048   100.5KB/s   00:00
```

rsync

rsync is an extremely versatile and efficient tool for synchronizing files and directories, either locally or between remote systems (often using SSH). Its key feature is that it only transfers the *differences* between the source and destination, making it much faster than `scp` for subsequent transfers if only small changes have occurred. It's a favorite for backups and mirroring data.

Basic Syntax (Remote Sync over SSH):

```
# Sync local directory contents TO remote directory
rsync -avz /path/to/local/source/
username@remote_host:/path/to/remote/destination/
```

```
# Sync remote directory contents FROM remote directory
rsync -avz username@remote_host:/path/to/remote/source/
/path/to/local/destination/
```

- -a: Archive mode (preserves permissions, ownership, timestamps, recurses into directories, etc.).
- -v: Verbose output.
- -z: Compress data during transfer.

rsync has many powerful options (like --delete to remove files at the destination that don't exist at the source) and is worth studying if you need robust file synchronization.

Downloading Files

Need to grab a file from the web directly from your terminal?

curl

curl (client **URL**) is a powerhouse for transferring data using various protocols (HTTP, HTTPS, FTP, SCP, etc.). It's widely used for testing web APIs, inspecting HTTP headers, and downloading files.

- **Download to stdout:** curl https://example.com/data.txt (Prints content to screen).
- **Save to file (-o or -O):**
    - curl -o local_filename.txt https://example.com/data.txt (Saves to local_filename.txt).
    - curl -O https://example.com/data.txt (Saves to a file named data.txt in the current directory, using the remote filename).
- **Follow redirects (-L):** curl -L https://short.link/resource

```
$ curl -O https://raw.githubusercontent.com/torvalds/linux/master/README
  % Total    % Received % Xferd  Average Speed   Time    Time     Time  Current
                                 Dload  Upload   Total   Spent    Left  Speed
100  1116  100  1116    0     0   5048      0 --:--:-- --:--:-- --:--:--  5049
$ ls README
README
```

wget

`wget` is specifically designed for robust, non-interactive file downloading from the web (HTTP, HTTPS, FTP).

- **Simple Download:** `wget https://example.com/archive.zip` (Saves to `archive.zip`).
- **Recursive Download (-r):** Can download entire websites (use with caution and respect `robots.txt`).
- **Resume Downloads (-c):** Can continue interrupted downloads.

```
$ wget https://ftp.gnu.org/gnu/bash/bash-5.2.tar.gz
--2024-07-24 11:05:10--  https://ftp.gnu.org/gnu/bash/bash-5.2.tar.gz
Resolving ftp.gnu.org (ftp.gnu.org)... 209.51.188.20, 2001:470:142:3::b
Connecting to ftp.gnu.org (ftp.gnu.org)|209.51.188.20|:443... connected.
HTTP request sent, awaiting response... 200 OK
Length: 11813496 (11M) [application/x-gzip]
Saving to: 'bash-5.2.tar.gz'

bash-5.2.tar.gz     100%[===================>]  11.27M  6.80MB/s    in 1.7s

2024-07-24 11:05:12 (6.80 MB/s) - 'bash-5.2.tar.gz' saved [11813496/11813496]

$ ls bash-5.2.tar.gz
bash-5.2.tar.gz
```

Choose `curl` for versatility and API interaction, `wget` for straightforward file downloading.

A Quick Introduction to Version Control with `git`

As you write more scripts, modify configuration files, or work on any text-based project, keeping track of changes becomes essential. What did that script look like yesterday before you made those "improvements"? How can you safely try out a new feature without messing up the working version? How can multiple people collaborate on the same set of scripts without overwriting each other's work? The answer is **Version Control Systems (VCS)**, and the undisputed standard today is `git`.

Why use `git` (even for personal projects)?

- **History Tracking:** `git` records snapshots (called **commits**) of your project over time. You can see who changed what, when, and why.
- **Reverting Mistakes:** Easily go back to any previous version of your files if you make a mistake or change your mind.
- **Branching and Merging:** Create separate lines of development (**branches**) to work on new features or fixes without affecting the main stable version. Later, you can merge your changes back.
- **Collaboration:** `git` is designed for distributed collaboration, allowing multiple people to work on the same project simultaneously and efficiently merge their contributions. Platforms like GitHub, GitLab, and Bitbucket provide hosting for `git` repositories.
- **Backup (of sorts):** While not its primary purpose, having your project history stored in `git` (especially when pushed to a remote repository) provides a form of backup.

Core `git` Concepts (Ultra-Simplified):

1. **Repository (Repo):** A directory containing your project files and a special hidden `.git` subdirectory where `git` stores the entire history and configuration. You create one using `git init` in your project directory.
2. **Working Directory:** Your actual project files that you edit.
3. **Staging Area (Index):** A temporary holding area where you prepare changes before committing them. You add files to the staging area using `git add <filename>`.
4. **Commit:** A snapshot of your project (specifically, the files in the staging area) at a particular point in time, stored permanently in the repository history with a descriptive message. You create a commit using `git commit -m "Your descriptive message"`.
5. **Branch:** An independent line of development. The default branch is usually called `main` or `master`. You create new branches with `git branch <branch_name>` and switch between them with `git checkout <branch_name>` (or `git switch <branch_name>` in newer versions).
6. **Remote:** A version of your repository hosted somewhere else (like GitHub). You add remotes using `git remote add <name> <url>`.
7. **Push:** Send your local commits to a remote repository (`git push <remote_name> <branch_name>`).
8. **Pull:** Fetch changes from a remote repository and merge them into your local branch (`git pull <remote_name> <branch_name>`).

Getting Started:

```
$ cd ~/playground/my_script_project # Go to your project directory
$ git init # Initialize a new git repository here
Initialized empty Git repository in
/home/jane/playground/my_script_project/.git/
$ # Create or edit your script(s), e.g., awesome_script.sh
$ git add awesome_script.sh # Stage the new script
$ git commit -m "Initial commit of awesome script" # Create the first snapshot
[main (root-commit) a1b2c3d] Initial commit of awesome script
 1 file changed, 50 insertions(+)
 create mode 100755 awesome_script.sh
$ # Make more changes...
$ git add awesome_script.sh # Stage the changes
$ git commit -m "Add error handling and logging" # Commit again
```

This is merely a tiny glimpse. Learning `git` properly involves understanding branching, merging, resolving conflicts, working with remotes, and much more. It requires dedicated practice and study (many excellent online tutorials, books, and resources exist). However, **start using `git` now**, even for your simple personal scripts stored locally. The benefits of having a history and the ability to undo mistakes are invaluable.

Where to Go From Here?

You've reached the end of the core path laid out in this book, but your Linux journey is really just beginning! The command line and scripting offer endless possibilities. Where you go next depends on your interests:

- **Deepen Shell Knowledge:** Explore more advanced Bash features like arrays in detail, more complex traps, subshells and process management nuances, coprocesses, shell parameter expansion tricks, and advanced scripting patterns.
- **Master Text Tools:** Dive deeper into `awk` programming, advanced `sed` techniques, and more intricate regular expressions.
- **Other Scripting Languages:** If your tasks become too complex for shell scripting (as discussed in Chapter 17), Python is an extremely popular and powerful choice on Linux, with extensive libraries for almost anything. Perl and Ruby are also strong contenders in the sysadmin space.
- **System Administration:** Learn more about managing users and groups, software package management (e.g., `apt`, `dnf`, `yum`), service management (`systemd`, `systemctl`), storage (filesystems, LVM, partitioning), networking configuration in depth, security hardening, and monitoring.

- **Specific Distributions:** Explore the unique tools, philosophies, and communities around distributions like Debian, Ubuntu, Fedora, CentOS/RHEL, Arch Linux, openSUSE, etc.
- **Containerization:** Learn about Docker or Podman for packaging applications and their dependencies into isolated containers, simplifying deployment and scaling.
- **Cloud & DevOps:** Explore how Linux dominates cloud computing platforms (AWS, Google Cloud, Azure) and the DevOps practices built around automation, infrastructure-as-code, and CI/CD pipelines, where shell scripting often plays a crucial role.
- **Kernel & Low-Level:** For the truly adventurous, delve into C programming and explore the Linux kernel itself.

Most Importantly: Practice! Apply what you've learned. Automate tasks in your daily workflow. Read other people's scripts. Don't be afraid to experiment (in safe environments like virtual machines or your `playground` directory). Join online communities, forums (like Stack Exchange sites, Reddit's Linux subreddits), or local Linux User Groups (LUGs) to ask questions and learn from others.

Chapter Summary / Book Conclusion

This chapter rounded out your toolkit by introducing essential utilities for working with **archives** (`tar`, `gzip`, `zip`), performing basic **networking** tasks (`ping`, `ip addr`, `ssh`, `scp`, `rsync`), and **downloading files** (`curl`, `wget`). We also highlighted the critical importance of **version control** and strongly encouraged you to start using `git` to track changes in your scripts and configurations. Finally, we pointed towards numerous exciting avenues for **further learning**, depending on your specific interests within the vast Linux ecosystem.

From the first `echo` command to writing automated, scheduled tasks, you've acquired a powerful set of skills. The Linux command line isn't just a relic of the past; it's a dynamic, efficient, and deeply rewarding environment for interacting with computers. Shell scripting allows you to bend that environment to your will, automating the mundane and building custom solutions.

www.ingramcontent.com/pod-product-compliance
Lightning Source LLC
LaVergne TN
LVHW062312060326
832902LV00013B/2182